LOVE LETTERS TO A STRIPPER

CREATE A FUTURE THAT WILL HAVE YOU DITCHING THE DESPERATION OF DANCING

Angelina Lombardo

McClean, Virginia, USA

Published 2018

DISCLAIMER

Cover Design: Jennifer Stimson
Editing: Todd Hunter
Author's photo courtesy of: Presley + Jude

ISBN: 9781683092339

TABLE OF CONTENTS

Hello you,

Strippers are humans. We need love too.

This entire book is my love letter to you.

To all of you beautiful souls, I see you, and I know who you truly are. You are beautiful, divine, lovingly made, and unbelievably powerful.

Embracing our darkest edges as humans is deep work. I consider it an honor to be a part of your journey.

I wrote this book for you and for the you who you would like to become. We are infinitely wise, and pure love is our destiny. My desire for you is to know that on a cellular level one that leaves no room for denial in the wisdom of your heart. My desire is for you to experience an awakening, the kind that ignites your passion and ignites a desire to create the life you can't wait to wake up to. My desire is that this discovery will feel undeniable to you and that you have every chance, and everything within you, to make this your reality.

My truest desire is for you to know that if you're searching for that one person in the world who will change your life, take a look in the mirror and like I discovered along my journey you will find that you are it, and it's been you all along.

I love you.
Angelina

FOREWORD
BY DR WAYNE D PERNELL

We all have stuff in our past that we want to shake off. Being human, we experience stress and even trauma and somehow make it through. While most of us don't endure true darkness, the pathway out is similar. We have our breakthroughs when we recognize our reality and want something better. And then, we commit to that focus on "better."

One might expect a dark memoire or an erotic expose from Angelina Lombardo's book, *Love Letters To A Stripper*. Instead, we're brought into the important work of self-preservation through self-reflection. The outcome is standing in one's strength.

When we are invited to peek behind the veil of an otherwise shrouded world, we tread with a voyeuristic interest and it is not uncommon to wonder if it is even okay to ask if the woman on the other side of that wide-open, yet closed-off world is okay.

The author normalizes – actually *humanizes* – the journey and as a reader, you might find yourself in a space of relative discomfort as we follow along in the process of shedding shame. This is a gritty, yet beautiful invitation.

Finding one's voice is a powerful journey. It is a path not easily followed and yet, when you decide to step back into your *self*, your true self, you let go of shame, you take back the power that you had let someone else hold for you for so long, and you embrace new choices in your life.

As you step into the space of choosing your power, you wonder why you let go of it in the first place. The shame cycle starts back up. Fortunately, the healing cycle runs in tandem. You are invited to trust again. And trusting in yourself before trusting in others is essential.

From the stories and personal anecdotes to the exercises and direct guidance, you'll find that *Love Letters To A Stripper* brings you back to that core self that had been hiding for so long. This time, that core self no longer needs the armor. Instead, it seeks to blossom forward.

Dr Wayne Pernell is an Amazon #1 International Best-Selling Author, and in-demand Speaker and Breakthrough Coach. For the past four decades, he has been helping thousands of people find their true voice and stand in their full being.

INTRODUCTION: OUR SECRET STRIP CLUB IN THE SKY

This book is for you if:

You wish things were different
You had turned left instead of right
You had said yes instead of no
You're feeling something calling to you, but you're not sure what it is
You're finding yourself restless, and nothing really calms you down
You aren't sure what you should be doing, but what you're doing now is not it
You're tired of using your power to endure unnecessary bullshit
You struggle reconciling your heart with your mind, while not quite fitting into the options that have come your way

Realize that you are not alone. You are unique, and you are *not* alone. Know that! Embrace it. Believe it, even though you think you have no reason to. Also, know that I will not be resolving these or any other mysteries for you. Instead, you will, later on in this book.

Don't worry, though. I'm not off on a yacht somewhere! I'm here for you, and while these words have been sitting on this page for a while, I'm yearning for a conversation and a connection with you. Imagine we're having a conversation even as you turn the pages of this book. I'll be sharing some of my story that I've held close for so long. I'm sharing it now, because while I've been a life coach, with my dancing past distant in the rearview mirror, part of my continued process of healing and self-evaluation revealed a call to meet my past as a stripper head on. I felt a strong need to connect with the dancing community and share my experience. I felt a strong need to be seen and heard and to be of service to those who are on the crossroads that I once traveled and to listen so that you can share your stories with me – without shame or judgment.

Our stories are human. We're human. We're not the misfits and outcasts society makes us to be. Still, until society is ready for us, we need to reach out and help each other. This book is a cozy chair where you can sit and consider who you are and where you're going. I'm the permission. It's also a safe place if you're of a mind to spill some secrets.

I'm going to ask a lot of you. I'm going to ask that you show compassion for yourself. I'm going to invite you to be my friendly witness and feel compassion for the very personal story that I'm about to share with you. I'm going to ask some tough questions and ask you to look deeply and honestly within yourself for the answers. I'm going to ask you to challenge yourself - to challenge some long-held beliefs, your reasons, your choices, and your process. I'm going to challenge your why. My hope is that some of these reasons become even more galvanizing as they withstand the storm of your challenge. My hope is that you'll audit and edit these reasons and that some will be replaced by new ones – all in alignment with who you are and who you are going to become. For you are always becoming, even if you decide not to change anything about yourself. You have to own that decision too.

Whether you're reading this book as an exotic dancer, curious about someone else's experience, or you're just intrigued by the story of how a stripper put her clothes back ON and ditched the shame and healed from a history of abuse, I know this book will be just the beginning of a deeper connection with yourself, a tighter alignment with that destiny charted by your stars, and a challenge that you will respond to with your heart, your flow, and your mojo – all wrapped inside the intriguing tale of a broke stripper.

SHAMETHROWER? FLAMETHROWER!

*"You may have lost hope floating in this sea of endless abyss
I am tossing a rope, grab onto it Beche!"*

—Angelina Lombardo

~

You have been dreaming of this day for weeks – no, years. You've come close a few times, but always talked yourself out of it. This time you're sure. You turn into the parking lot, coming in hot, Kendrick blaring.

You park farther away from the entrance than you need to, so you can get up to swag speed on your strut to the door. You are surprisingly loose, even high-fiving your least favorite bartender, who's drying stemware.

The club is slow, as expected at 3:15 p.m. on a Thursday. On your way to the back office, you drop into the dressing room for a few hugs. You grab a robe and put it on over your outfit – a silk mandarin collar top and shredded jeans – and head for the door. It's open as usual, and you lean into the doorway and calmly state your three little words. With a wry smile, you turn around and head back down the hallway. Just one more trip across the stage left.

As the dull sound of Bodak Yellow pounds through the dark main room, you get up on the empty stage. You shimmy for the few patrons who are probably ditching work, and make a show of taking off your robe. As a barely noticeable catcall of encouragement echoes throughout the room, you announce to the sparse crowd, "It's been real, but I am OUT, bitches!"

The robe billows as it slowly whisps its way to the floor, and you bound directly off the stage, flickering dual deuces as you head out the entrance into the blinding light.

You glide over the asphalt back to your car and peel out - though the only sound you hear, over the tires screeching, and the music blaring, was that of your soul applauding.

~

Take a moment to savor whatever version of your escape that you've been dreaming.

Celebrate the rebel in you, the rebel who decided that dancing would be your way to make ends meet and kept you safe in a sea of exploitation and shame.

Now, put that rebel away. You'll need her for the work you need to do, much more important work than that cinematic resignation that sweetly rescued you from the leering, the sporadic pay, and the toxicity oozing off clients and co-workers alike. It's time to go to work!

Why did you start dancing? Was it a slow, deliberate decision or an impulsive one? What were your expectations, once you started? How different was reality from those expectations? I'll share my story in the next chapter but know that I understand that there are many reasons you might have for making that choice and reasons for why you are making a change. I'm here to support you where you're at now and where you dream you will be in your future.

No judgement. Seriously!

I want you to trust me. I believe you will feel in your gut the authenticity with which I share my message and that it will become very clear that I not only understand your pain and struggle but also have successfully tread this path and attained a life that I had dreamt of having. If I can do it, so can you!

I have had an ongoing issue with trust myself. I have had to do some very hard work to enjoy the gifts of what trust brings to my life. In my past when meeting people for the first few times, I found myself testing them in a variety of ways to see if they were worth having close. I was mostly unconscious of this at the time but I needed to know if they were safe – truly safe. I have abuse in my past, so most people who have been in my life were not safe. I was often confused.

I have earned 100-percent trust in myself now – that's the only thing that changed.

I have not only used but live my life currently based on all of the philosophies and personal perspectives I discuss in this book, and I have learned over the years working on myself that trust isn't something that happens when someone proves to you that they are trustworthy. It's an inside job first - when you can trust yourself, it's almost natural to start seeing trust develop for others.

I want you to know that not only do I understand that but, also I am here for you. I will handle, hold, and love you through your difficult rebellious, hard-edged responses.

Again, when it comes to your choices, I am not here to pass judgment, tell you that I know better or tell you what you have to do or how you should do it. I know I am the window, and you are the light. Let's get that straight.

I for sure don't ever fucking want to suggest that you should, could, or would be a better person if you did; that shit is not accurate anyway. When I got into the game, it was out of desperation. I had no home; I couldn't feed myself. I was living for "someone" outside of myself to care for me: people I didn't know, the welfare system, or friends overburdened with my homelessness. I also felt just plain good old-fashion shame at not being able to support myself. When I started dancing, I quickly felt empowered, which led to confusion, shame, and hiding.

When I started making money, after attempting desperately to find employment – legitimate employment – I was terrified and liberated at the same time. It provided a freedom I had never experienced or known about. All of a sudden, I could pay for rent and food; I made my own hours. It allowed me to have the freedom to be fucked up in the head, and if I couldn't get around my mental illness, I didn't have to work on those days. I could stretch what little money I did have until I could coax myself back into taking my clothes off.

I would not in a million years pass judgment. I am one of you; we are all sisters. We are all powerful beyond measure, and we are all capable of whatever we dream, desire, and envision. I am just here to hold space for you until you can walk right on past me in your full fucking color-blinding, blazing glory! I was put here on the planet with a service-oriented heart. I am coming back to scoop up whoever wants to come with me. I have surpassed shit I never thought I could.

I can for sure roll back in the timeline of life and recall who, what, and where I have come from, and who was rolling right next to me. Typically, they weren't reliable, trustworthy, good intentioned souls – they were dysfunctional in their own ways and seemed to fit with just how lost and confused I was. Ultimately, I was blessed with a full spectrum of relationships and had experiences with some pretty amazing people, and that stimulated my desire to forge ahead and continue my search for health and balance.

Midwifery was one of my favorite career paths.

In my days of working with pregnant mothers, coming from all backgrounds and walks of life, there was one thing that I would communicate with them during our first meeting: "This is some of the most intimate work you will ever do in life, and you will remember me for the rest of your life. If you don't vibe with me or can't be honest with yourself or me, this won't work. I am asking you to trust me, but it will never be for myself. I need your trust so that you can have the birth that you want."

I'm asking you to trust me so that I can be the best partner, the best witness, the best supporter of whatever unique, magical shit you need to go through to get what you want.

My wish for you is to realize your version of success health and balance. Your best chance for that is by getting out of your own way as much as possible. So let's talk about one of the most common self-sabotaging actions that you, along with millions of others, have most likely experienced: hiding.

Something has got to be said about our hiding – you, me, and the world around us (even other people in other cultures on the globe of this planet hide).

It isolates in such a deep and insidious way that the sense is we are all alone forever and ever more, but the truth is so much more gentle than our thoughts. Reality is kinder than our thoughts.

Being seen and heard, being open, can often be a daunting experience. Yet more than anything, being seen and heard is a primal desire deep within us. Our silent, shrinking, hiding selves retreat because we often come across the harshness of critics and doubters who douse our creativity, right when we are most vulnerable.

We learn to lock away this voice, thinking we are protecting it – but it withers in the drought of our doubts. Perhaps we even start to think that if we let this shadow out, it would alienate us, unaware that these reservations prevent us from finding our community.

We are more alike than different, yet we rarely touch this awareness because we practice at excluding ourselves. To varying degrees, we all split our soul-life off from the face we share in public. But perhaps more insidious is how we distance ourselves from those aspects of the self that are devalued in our families and culture.

Additionally, due to the work we chose – or that chose us – we are beckoned to hide even deeper. Sometimes we can't even understand the confusion and shame in our decisions that caused our hiding.

Are you hiding? In what ways do you know you are hiding? Are those ways taking from you? Do you feel a sense of doom and urgency for help? Has depression paid you a visit? The truth is, shame and depression run in the same crowd, and they take down the meek and the mighty.

When we're immersed in shame, it's all too easy to let the projections of how society views us to filter in. Even when we've carved out this life through empowerment and inner strength, the taboos and labels are relentless, and creating armor to shut it out creates other problems – chiefly, what of our close relationships? How do they deal with the taboos and labels, and how do you deal with their handling of it? You will need to account for the extra energy to help bring them along – you can't afford to wait for our culture to catch them up.

The reality of the dancing game isn't just about shame, though. That's just the entry fee. It's a reality that you have to constantly address, but it isn't the only one. The fallout from dancing for money isn't something you can easily put a dollar value on, because the consequences aren't always apparent or measurable.

It's a daily struggle - one moment you are juggling everything perfectly, and the next you're a volcanic eruption and can't possibly hold it all together. Working wacky hours, dealing with the creepy clientele or cattiness or drama from other dancers, and playing games to ensure you have the support of bartenders and bouncers when you need it all take their toll. This doesn't even take into account the real damage you are doing to your body, spending its best years on people who don't give a shit about you beyond their objectification.

It's no wonder the doubts creep in!

You don't get nearly enough money to cover for all of the compromises you're making. You likely made this decision based on the money you'd be getting but had no idea how much money it would be costing to pay the club and keep your body right, and how much damage it would be doing. You thought this would be a subway stop on your way to your "real" career – but now you're not sure how or if you can leave, or what you can do.

I've seen young people taken by the pitfall of thinking they will dance as a temporary fix to earn a college or vocational degree or the equivalent.

Consider Tina, who wants to take herself outta the workforce and learn a trade so that she can make a living wage doing something she thinks will be good for herself, her future, and humanity. She is thinking that nursing is her way. She is twenty-four years old and has already been exposed to the struggles of living on her own. She attended public school and was the first to graduate high school in her family. She's from a blue-collar family, and there is no shortage of financial struggles in her family's experience of the American dream, so they can't help her pay for school. Tina wants to do better for her future and believes part of that is getting an education.

21

Tina decides to start dancing to gain the money for college. At first, she's surprised at the money she's making and is convinced she made the right choice. Then she starts realizing that she has trouble focusing at school on the mornings after she works at the club. She might have enough hours in the week to do both, but she can't choose her schedule. She switches from being a full-time to part-time student.

Eventually, she drops out of school entirely, and while it didn't start out that way, her decision to start dancing has created a rift among her future, her reality, and her inner compass and personal integrity.

It's absolutely critical to ensure you're always aligned with your own values and priorities and not look at legitimizing yourself by external measures.

Back to Tina: She has decided to quit dancing and go back to school. She gets her RN degree and is working as an intern for a few months, but she is struggling to pay the rent on her entry-level salary. After a few weeks of looking for a second job, she decides to go back to dancing for a while, just to supplement her income. Maybe it'll be better at the next club.

See how the cycle is hard to break, when you use external values – in this case, money – as a signal for what you should be doing? And your internalized shame – not knowing what's best for you – has you tricked and trapped. Its message is "You're doing something wrong; you are the problem."

You are also in danger of wearing other people's shit stories about who strippers are perceived to be. Wearing these is not your responsibility. These stories don't belong with you. Power and agency are too easily given up without your awareness. You need to understand this so that you are free to make your own informed choices.

The real danger comes when you take on this shame as your own. You may have enough of your own unowned shame – don't accept any that's thrust on you, whether it's based on a co-worker dealing with drama, society's stigmas, abuse from your past, or from family and friends struggling to accept you for who you really are. This shame creates thoughts that zap your energy and can emotionally charge you in a way that it's hard not to react.

While sticking it out in the stripper game might seem enticing – there's some gratification, clout, and energy from dancing and the money you can earn – the drawbacks are tough to deal with. You can be so busy fighting the obvious battles of respect, safety, and dignity that you don't even notice the damage that the slinking, lurking demons of shame, exploitation, and discrimination are causing. What's worse, is that this stuff can stick around, poking its head out at the most inconvenient times.

I want to talk openly about shame, power, choice, and options. I want to share with you the process I've used to heal myself, accept and embrace my inner voice, and chart my own course based on what I want, not based on what others think I can do. I've also refined this process in discussion with my clients, and I can't wait to start sharing it with you.

First, though, I'd like to share my story.

A LIGHT IN THE DARK

"If what I say resonates with you,
it is merely because we are both branches from the same tree."
—W. B. Yeats

I danced, defiantly. I danced out of desperation. I danced into
discord and drama. I danced to fucking survive. It was an
obvious choice, and I was ready for it. Powerful and independent,
confidently sexual, I easily put on my costume of nudity for the
creeps sleeping in their leering leisure.
I danced, and I was not at all ready for it. The lewd attention would
have disembodied me, if the sexual abuse in my past hadn't gotten
me there first. The shitload of shame should have made me shudder,
but it was already there, too fucking familiar.
I danced as a detour from my homelessness. It worked.

I was raised in Australia to sexual, physical, verbal, emotional, psychological, and mental abuse, which plagued my young soul. I hid. I tried fitting in. I tried isolating myself. I thought, for a long, long time, that the pain and abuse were normal and that I was the problem. I moved to Arizona when I was thirteen. I realized I could no longer tolerate or accept the abuse. I had a rare moment of hope when one of the few people who believed in me and was willing to act helped plan my rescue attempt. I was inconsolable and crestfallen when it fell through at the last minute and stumbled into nomadic homelessness when I was fourteen.

I was hospitalized for depression several times. I was committed twice to a psychiatric hospital. I lived in a girls' home, lived with foster families, and couch surfed with friends and strangers alike. I attempted suicide four times and was almost successful two times. I have died twice. One attempt landed me in a coma for two weeks; the other damaged my liver for the rest of my life. I was drinking and doing whatever drugs I could to kill myself. I possessed a gripping self-hatred. I was twice a victim of rape. I hid, in plain sight.

I fled to Maui when I was eighteen. It certainly didn't make all of the pain go away – but it was a major choice that I made, for me. I had jobs, even some good ones, but some reason would always come up for me to leave. I had started various attempts at being an entrepreneur, but nothing stuck. So I danced. It started insidiously, couched in a way that made it feel like no big deal. It morphed from private dances to dancing in a club, and I danced my way through parties, money, broke, and the sticky shame of a day after that needed more than a tub soak to shake off. I had a boyfriend from Israel, my first true love, who supported my dancing. That seemed and sounded empowering. I went to Israel with him and witnessed the normalization of war.

I came back to Maui. I hid as if it were my shame to bear. I hid from stories put on me. Someone else's regurgitated version of life experience. I hid from judgment, being misunderstood, not being heard, and being crushed by that experience! I could no longer sustain anyone else's story of me. Who were they to think they knew better about my interior world than me? I had the view, but I was so busy trying to be heard or seen or understood that quite honestly I didn't understand myself anymore, and I sure was not in touch with who I was, where I was, or why. Sure I had stories, but answers? I had answers for everyone else, but not for myself, my most important person – I had none. I had no direction. I was waving in the wind like a flower in a field, going wherever the wind took me, unaware that I alone could create that experience for me. I was unaware that it was not just destiny but how I showed up in the world that would create my beautiful unfolding journey!

I needed to escape, really. The horrors I had already experienced were more than enough for one lifetime. They do not get to write my story. So much of my life was handed down to me and ignorantly accepted. I eventually gained the awareness that I was unknowingly giving my power away, that too much energy was being spent on allowing other people to place their stories onto me. I am the rightful owner of this human experience.

I met my daughter's father through dancing and went from one dysfunction almost overnight into another one. My daughter was, and remains to this day, the sweetest and most grounding part of my life. I attempted to endure abuse to try to give her some of the things that I never had: a taste of so-called normal, a sense of stability. It was not in the cards, though. The abuse was too prevalent and did not just stop at me. So I left and took my daughter with me, despite threats of repercussions. I was a great mother, and I knew we were each other's best chances, and I was determined to chart a different course for my daughter, so I left.

I tried so many jobs – bookkeeping, real estate, selling time-shares, carpet cleaning, being a personal assistant, running vacation rentals, becoming a chef and a midwife – trying to find a way out, a way back, a way to support my daughter and me and stay afloat.

~

I danced again. I danced again, out of desperation, again. I danced again, for my daughter's dinners. I danced again, from domestic violence into disaster.

I danced again, and that was one of the bullshit reasons my daughter was taken from me.

~

It didn't dawn on me that they would take my baby. He had threatened to, but conventional wisdom was that the mother rarely loses custody, and he was often an uninterested and abusive father. We had been on our own for months, making it work. I had returned to dancing, but I was convinced it was on my terms this time. I was focused on providing for my daughter and was a wonderful nurturing mother. Everyone knew it. He knew it.

His pride, his money, his reputation as a professional athlete, the patriarchal structure that runs strongly in Hawaii, and the stigma associated with dancing said otherwise, however. I will never – never – forget the night they forcibly took her from my arms, law enforcement playing a role despite there being no direction from the court yet. I felt like I never had a real chance, that the odds were stacked too heavily against me. It was a devastation different from any other. Being a mother helped focus my energy on being different than those values and suffering that I'd experienced – and while that wasn't the same as healing, it was what I was holding on to.

~

I ditched dancing, to get my daughter back. I ditched dancing to discovery, healing, and debilitating disease.

～

I kept dancing for a little while, but I knew it was just a matter of time before I left again. I had some doubt that I would find something, but that only set me back for a little while. I just decided, one day, not to show up for work. I had moved on. I resolved to find a way – any way – to get my daughter back. In the end, his disinterest, another child from another mother, and my persistence – brought her back to me. Just when I truly believed I was un-empowered, I found my edge, and there was no other way but through! The way out is through.

I got my Realtor's license and started working in real estate. I worked with several people and quickly saw how interconnected so many other services were to the buying and selling of property: staging, marketing, financing, insurance, underwriting. I understood the process end to end and am very good at seeing the whole picture and jumping in where I can do the most good. I found through the staging part of the process that I was great at cleaning and organizing, so I entered the wonderful world of working while listening to music at ear-blasting volumes, and eventually, my own cleaning business was born.

I was also beginning to show signs of the healing work I had been doing.

I was well on my path of building my cleaning empire when I felt the first signs of trouble. It started with a lack of energy. As you can imagine, having recently gotten my daughter back, I was not about to let some little shit derail my train at this moment. I pressed on, not even considering slowing down. But it just got worse. It wasn't until I passed out on the job and was coerced by my real- life guardian angel to seek medical attention for whatever was draining me.

But doctors couldn't help. A bunch of doctors, a ton of treatment, and eventually, international travel to find the best care still didn't provide any answers. It took a hot minute – over a year – before it was finally diagnosed as Lyme's disease, which helped to put a name on it, but it was only a superficial answer. Lyme's produces myriad complications and a mile-long list of symptoms and can often have lingering effects. In addition to chronic fatigue, I have suffered and still struggle with joint and muscle pain and memory loss. I am challenged daily from a health perspective.

I spent ten years of my life coordinating, recovering, rewiring, parenting, learning, "driving" my life – all from a bed. As extremely challenging as this period of my life was, and while I was often forced to surrender and let go of my plans and expectations, I realized that I'd said goodbye to desperation – that cruel bitch. I had healed enough to begin to have confidence in myself. Not that I had all of the answers – but that I could find them, just me. I was strong enough to stick up for myself, and strong enough to accept my imperfections. This accelerated so much processing of my past. I was able to understand, accept, and love the lost girl and recognize and welcome her as a part of me.

I'd also like to confide that *Law & Order SVU* has some seriously therapeutic mojo, and I leveraged all of that goodness during my time in bed. Seeing that not only were there people out there who had experienced trauma, abuse, and suffering, but also that there were people out there who were willing to help, to see, to not forget: this held so much value for me, and it is probably not surprising that as I grew as a life coach, this became one of my foundational elements.

I'm sharing my dancing story to shake off the rest of the shame. It's sticky and slimy, and it's not even all mine. I'm sharing my story to be seen and heard and to serve and heal. I'm sharing my story to answer my call to connect. I'm sharing my story so we can find each other.

I was well on my journey as a life coach, in service to others, after having experienced healing, empowerment, and recovery in my own life. I thought I was doing what I was called to do, until I experienced several events and revelations in close succession. First, my mother, a cocreator of a large amount of my childhood trauma, died the summer of 2017, a day before my birthday. While I had undergone so much healing and acquired a strong sense of self, I was not really aware until she died that I was still in some part aware of the cage that she'd created, even if I was no longer captive. My mom's death released me from the sense that I wasn't in true ownership of my direction, of charting my own course. I had taken profound steps in healing, transforming, and acknowledging my sense of self but only now realized that I had not closed the cage door behind me when I escaped and only now grasped as the bars, and the cage, evaporated.

Next, my mother's ex-husband, who had molested me throughout my childhood, attempted to reach out to me via social media, just as I was starting to use those platforms for my coaching business for outreach and to support my current and past clients. This led to a sense of apprehension and a perceived threat that triggered an emotional response to protect and a subsequent protective desire to withdraw. I didn't think I was ready to leverage a platform that left me so open and accessible. I worked internally on my reaction and came to an understanding that I was not only ready but also needed to embrace and be willing to engage – and be vulnerable to – any and all platforms that would allow me to reach my audience, wherever they are, and allow me to be seen and heard – secure in myself and the work that I've done and free of fear of what others could or would do to me, intentionally or not.

Lastly, the #MeToo movement was encouraging, intoxicating, and exciting: people, largely women, were sharing their experiences of sexual assault and abuse. This certainly led to a shift in cultural awareness, an outpouring of support, and a debate and dialogue about safety, support, predators, and victimhood. My reaction was initially to withdraw; this was something personal to me, and I was aware of the depth of trauma and the work it took me to gain my equilibrium and health reclaiming my personal power. This movement seemed to take away the very personal ownership of my experience.

Eventually, I came to realize that letting go of my attachment to my childhood/young adulthood abuse not only gave me permission to show up unapologetically in my coaching practice but also, by seeing my limited belief for what it was, I was now ready to be the example for my future clients.

I found that the confluence of these events triggered the awareness that I wanted to embrace my past and work directly with the exotic dancer audience. Having several years of coaching under my belt left me ready to identify and accept this calling that previously had been too triggering, too close.

After being a victim of domestic violence and the subsequent loss of custody of my daughter because of the shame and judgment associated with being an exotic dancer, I was determined to end the cycle of violence, victimhood, disempowerment, and shame in my life once and for all for my daughter. Through healing, I understood and answered my call to service through life coaching.

As I continued my journey, I began to realize that the larger call was to reach out to serve not only the exotic dancer community but also the larger community of those who should be our support in a world free of shame, and to cast light on the seedy systems that enable that shame and are complicit in it. While it does suck that these systems use shame to isolate dancers (a.k.a you and me) from society, it's an unfortunate problem that will take longer to solve and comes with the territory. In the meantime, it can be helpful to understand and have patience for those family and friends who have been brainwashed by these social stigmas. It's also important to understand that we aren't going to wait for the systems we should have, or the relationship support we deserve, to arrive. We're making the change happen, here and now. And one step at a time, we'll eventually bring the rest of them with us. This book is the first part of that.

3

FROM THE ASHES, A BLINGED-OUT SPIRAL STAIRCASE WRAPPED AROUND A DANCING POLE

Tough Love

You are not
some holiday destination
for people to have
a good time in,
and then forget.

You are not a grave
for people to bury
their pain inside,
never to be
remembered again.

You are made of magic,
don't you dare
allow yourself
to be treated
like you are any less.

—Nikita Gill

Throughout this book, I share some pretty intimate things about my life and my experiences, I have been banged up for sure but I am still 100% bad ass, those experiences made my "life swag" stronger!

I have taken my "dark nights of the soul" and used them as opportunities.

I have learned over the years from some great mentors and through a lot of personal grit, to bring all I have to each moment, to make it count. It's all we have, truly, we are not guaranteed the next.

Most importantly, I need you to bring it. Well, we both do. You need to bring it like your life depends on it. Because it does, sister! You need to attack this with all of the fierceness that's within you. We know it's there, because it's helped you get this far, for fuck's sake. But I'm not just talking about the mental side here. I need you to bring your body into this too. That's right, that sweet, strong temple that houses all of that heart, spirit, shame, doubt, thoughts – so many thoughts – and your breath.

Breathe. Seriously, right now. Just breathe deeply. I'm going to ask you to do that periodically, and I don't care where you're reading this, or who's around – when we talk about breathing, you really need to fucking do it. Deeply. Find your breath. If you already know it, you know how important it is in getting you ready to receive and direct your energy. If you're not sure whether you've found your breath or not – we'll get to it, don't worry! Just know that for now, I want you to acknowledge that you are a connected, powerful being, and that like a lot of complex systems, it's really hard to operate efficiently in one area if another is in distress.

I believe wholeheartedly that if you want access to your personal vault of power, you need to be right within your body, mind, and soul. I have structured this book to reflect this. I touch on each of these cornerstones, and it is of utmost importance that I make it clear. If you are out of balance in one of these areas, you will feel it in different ways. I believe the body informs the mind, and the soul is at the base of that experience. These informed aspects of your being can most definitely get hijacked by the mind.

Whether you think you have an arsenal full of super-powerful mind control, understand that your mind is wired to sabotage that false belief. It's not made for your control, it's made for your surrender. And it's your belief in your personal will that comforts you when your thinking creates drama. If it's not understood and in balance, it steals the show. You gotta know what's going on all up in there in order to pull the reins and achieve your desired outcome in any situation. Being the observer of your thoughts versus being your thoughts is a very important distinction to make. If you are able to identify that you are in fact not your thoughts, you can start to play around with creating your reality. And that is such good fucking news.

So now that you know about the mind-set I want you to bring, I'm going to sketch out my process for helping you get ready for change, it's a process because we first need to get you aligned, understanding, and feeling into the inner you before we create goals and sketch out a plan for you to achieve them.

Before I share with you what the rest of the book is about, I'm going to explain the framework I use when talking about the systems within you and how you can tap into them to understand yourself better.

INNER AUTHORITY COUNCIL

You get a multitude of information from a variety of sources and process and retain it in different ways. I like to refer to these components as your Inner Authority Council. They work together to help you understand what you want, what you need, and how to achieve your goals, keep yourself safe, interact with other people, deal with stress, and make decisions. They comprise your essence: the fibrous, elusive, nebulous stuff that makes you unique and determine who you showed up on this planet to be.

Sitting on the board of your Inner Authority Council are the following heavy hitters:

- Essential Self – who you are no matter the customs and social mores of your culture
- Felt Sense/Body wisdom – the systems, instincts, and behaviors that serve as receptors to your environment, and can also signal back to you their innate and insanely accurate perspective on what's right for you
- Emotional Intelligence – the ability to translate what you feel into understandable states that fuel your emotional engine
- Social Self – the part of you that's trained to interact and harmonize with your tribe, your culture, your environment. Sometimes, in trying to streamline these interactions, it will trample on your Essential Self. Consider yourself warned

I will often refer to various members of your council as appropriate throughout this book. Understand that while these individual parts of you are all important, it's up to you to ensure that they are balanced and doing right by you. It's especially obvious when one of these components is over- or underdeveloped. Someone with an overdeveloped social self will often hide or suppress his or her Essential Self in order to fit in. Someone with an underdeveloped Social Self will appear awkward at interacting or extremely selfish or oblivious. Someone who's not tapped into their emotional intelligence might overreact under pressure or be unable to connect with others in an empathetic way.

The remainder of this book is focused on the processes for identifying and understanding yourself and teaching you how to identify what you truly want and how to get it.

Here's the Inside Work to connect with your Inner Authority:

- Mind Work
- Feeling into Your Body
- Understanding Your Emotions
- Awareness

I'll share some tips, strategies, and perspectives on how to prepare yourself for the start of your journey. It's definitely focused on setting you up for success, and how to get in the proper mind-set for setting yourself up for work that changes your life.

MIND WORK

After that short introduction, we'll focus with an intention of listening and understanding your mind. Your mind can definitely be one of your strongest assets, but unsurprisingly, our minds can often sabotage us in key ways: by either thinking your thoughts run the show, or by copying learned behaviors from our culture or family that are often not aligned with what we really want or need. I'll show you some techniques for quieting your mind and then understanding how it can be rewired and leveraged as the asset it should be.

FEELING INTO YOUR BODY

Then we'll segue to focus on our bodies: feeling into ourselves, and learning to trust that feeling as the truest compass we have. Just as our minds are often – culturally or environmentally – overused and are a source of interference, the sensations in our bodies are typically underdeveloped and misunderstood. You will learn to identify and leverage the sensations in your body, and why you're better off letting them steer your god pod or that divine body of yours.

UNDERSTANDING EMOTIONS

Next, we'll work on understanding our emotions, how to honor and respect those emotions, and learn how to figure out what they are telling us and just what to do with them. Too often emotions are identified with irrationality, when we should be using them as critically important information.

AWARENESS

The last part of the book will address how to take that enlightened awareness of your mind, body, and spirit and apply it through a process that supports your safety, growth, and change – and it's a process that you can use often and in every facet of your life.

- Understanding Your Needs, Values, and Choices
- Establishing Boundaries
- Taking Care of Yourself
- Dealing with Obstacles
- Sustain and Repeat – After Care

This book will then delve into the body, self-awareness, and some good old-fashioned self-care – because who else is going to do it? I'm only slightly joking – a well-worn scrap of crazy-ass-zen-wisdom states that to take care of others, we must first seek to take care of ourselves.

Of course, since we've both been through some shit, we know that no true plan for our future will survive unless we know how to handle some rough seas – so I'll show you some obstacles and some strategies for pushing through them.

Lastly, I'll discuss aftercare – what to do after you put this book down, plan in place. You'll know where to get help, when to call the hotline, and how to keep calm when everything goes wrong – because you've prepared for it, you have a plan, and it's nothing you can't deal with.

A HAMMOCK OF WOVEN G-STRINGS

"Those who love you are not fooled by mistakes you have made or dark images you hold about yourself. They remember your beauty when you feel ugly; your wholeness when you are broken; your innocence when you feel guilty; and your purpose when you are confused."

—Alan Cohen

Here we are. You decided you were curious enough to read past the cover of this book and now you are well on your way on a most interesting journey into investing in your personal economy, or you're just curious about the life of a broke stripper. Before we can go any further, I need you to know a few more things about me. And I will ask a few things of you. I want you to have a sense of who I showed up to be on the planet beyond my story.

I tried to fight, ignore, and outsmart Lyme's disease. I spent hours, energy, and money trying to push through. Ultimately, the lesson that has had the most lasting effect was surrender. Knowing how and when to let go. Letting go in this moment, when nothing was working, allowed my body to show me the way back. The benefits of surrender weren't done showing me their power though. Surrender helped me heal in so many other ways and allowed me to confront and defeat demons I had only previously been able to suppress, avoid, or ignore.

From acquiring a sharp shooter skill of surrendering, I have become a fierce force of nature. I am a true wild woman, a shadow walker, a cultivator of roots, a shapeshifter, an alchemical artist, an outlier, a pioneer woman. I am a daring, bold force to be reckoned with, an empirical existentialist, an absolutely attuned weaver of truth, and an angsty lover of shadows – all of this from my game with surrender.

Then there is the personal freedom gold mine that I have attained, freedom from the shame and sabotage that used to accompany making mistakes and trying to be perfect. I never again will apologize for who I am. Our focus must reside on accountability to ourselves not on justifying why we are who we are. Truth is, we fucking rock. Period.

I want to hold space with complete empathy, compassion, and fierceness for your highest self to be known in every moment!

I know you must be able to relate. It takes a huge amount of power and presence to get naked and tantalize other people's senses into a fantasy world that breeds the kind of distraction and destruction that we are all becoming ever so increasingly aware of. For your own good – it's beneficial that you know now, if you didn't already – it also breeds energy suckers. You are an unbelievable force to be reckoned, and I know this! I know that you are powerful and independent.

If you do not understand something in this book, the cool thing is, you can ask contact me here at angelinalombardo.com/lets-talk.

I am here for connection and that begins with a conversation. Books used to be about a solo adventure, and some still are. This book is different.

TRUST AND SAFETY

As you dive deeper into this book, and into yourself, I'd like you to trust yourself as well. We have layers and shells that we learn from society, or put in place to protect ourselves – but underneath it all, there is a voice, a feeling, trying to steer you. To find that voice, identify what it's telling you, and trust that it will take practice and commitment.

I believe you are brave. I will ask you to be brave. Real brave. Braver than you may think you can be. Brave like you are fighting for your life. PSSSSST here's a secret: you are, in fact, fighting for your life. The right to what you were given at birth, just for showing up as a human. The right to own every last inch of who you are and what you want to choose to do with that energy you possess on the daily. Life force is your energy force and it's one of the most important commodities that you own (in your human experience).

I am an experienced, compassionate warrioress, and I will be your defender, your co-creator, and also simply your friendly witness. Little did you know that you are being dragooned into a sisterhood that you will be so grateful to be a part of. There are many women in this sisterhood – they may or may not take their clothes off for a living, but they bare their souls in many of the same unconscious ways that we did and do. And many of them have found their right life, or are in their process of finding it.

Let's get back to this concept of a friendly witness: A friendly witness is someone who is safe to talk to and knows how to listen empathetically. They provide a space for your potentiation, whether the goal is to transform thoughts, concepts, beliefs, or just expressing your emotions. It is an extremely "self"-centered exercise for your inner wisdom. It's a phenomenon – you're one person when you start, and a different one when you're finished. Everyone needs a friendly witness, but not everyone has one!

SURRENDER — SHUT YOUR FUCKING MOUTH, SOCIAL SELF!

I need your commitment and dedication, after all if you don't have that, then what do you have? It has to be worth it to you to make the changes you want to make too. Don't worry – it's all for your own benefit. It's for you. Your biggest work. Your biggest love. Your biggest challenge. I want you to birth yourself. And then life will ask of you the same, many times over.

Each time you accept this, it will become easier and more clear, and you will have learned and attained the very crucial skill of breathing into your body to not only cope with your confusion in this moment but to prepare for the obstacles that lie in front of you.

You will be so skilled at playing this game of life that it won't slow you down ever again.

Even when death comes for you, you will come in barreling with fire at your back and the confidence to meet that inevitability with fervor. It sounds like a bunch of bullshit, but it's not.

Commitment to yourself and to your process is what I will ask of you. It was asked of me; the universe came calling, and I really couldn't say no.

Consciously, I went kicking and punching and flipping the fuck outta the sky. But the great mystery that be dragged me off, and into the underbelly of society I went.

My personal cocoon was hermetically sealed so that nothing extraneous could enter into my process. No projections could be made on it, no introduced doubt or criticism could reach it during its critical formative stages. I had already stacked and stored and hoarded enough shit from outside sources. It was time to prepare for the long haul.

But it was also sealed for my own good so that I didn't have an easy out. This is what's meant by "holding the tension." So in times of exhaustion and suffering, fear and frustration, we remain committed long enough for the process to complete itself. It was absolutely grueling, reminiscent of Jon Snow in *Game of Thrones* making his trek to the North. He knew it was his destiny to make that journey, though he did not know what the outcome would be.

THE GOLD MINE INSIDE

So, have you ever experienced magic? True magic – something that just trips your mind, and you're left wondering, *How the fuck did they do that?* It might even get your head throbbing as you try to rewind it, looking for the secrets, hidden in plain sight. It might be some kind of performance art, like a magician or a *Cirque du Soleil* show, or something mystical, or some wonder you experience out in nature. You might even wish that you could do something like that or ponder what your life would be like if you could do that.

What would you change in your life if you possessed magical powers? Seriously, write something down.

Whether you've witnessed such a kind of magic or not, know that some of the truest, most pure magic that you could ever come across resides right there, inside of you.

OK, so here's the hardest part. Seriously. To really connect with yourself, to identify more deeply with who you were meant to be, you have got to surrender. You've got to relinquish control from your mind. Surrender your thoughts about who you are, who you should be, how you should get there. Surrender your expectations of how other people should treat you. Allow everything to just be.

I could talk forever about surrender, and how important it is, but that would be boring! For simplicity, let's just start with 3 core concepts that will represent surrender for this book:

- Accept yourself
- Embrace your experience – the bad and the good
- Trust your inner-self

The core concept of accepting yourself means opening up and making room for the difficult feelings, urges, and sensations – allowing them to "flow" through you without struggle. You don't have to like or want these feelings – you just make room for them and allow them to be there even though they are unpleasant. At least once a day, practice breathing into and making room for difficult feelings and sensations.

So what does it mean to surrender? Well, I'm not asking you to just plop down in the nearest river and let the current take you away! I want you to consider surrender as a simmering stew, consisting of the following savory ingredients:

- Let your mind be quiet and take a back seat
- Let go of your expectations on who you are and what you should be
- Consider concepts that are uncomfortable; challenge your current beliefs
- Identify your essence outside of your environment and the one you were raised in

With these aspects of surrender in mind, take a critical look at the relationship between your Essential Self and your Social Self. Most of us have designed a life based on our Social Selves, not based on our Essential Selves. The Social Self is who we think we should be, based on the customs and cultural norms of our environment and key individuals in our life.

If we've designed a life based on our Social Self, we often find ourselves dissatisfied. We walk around wishing that life was different, that we felt different, that we lived with peace and passion.

These two have to be on the same page and especially in the same country! If they are at odds it's a perpetual shit storm of crappy consequences and pretty soon, you won't recognize your life because it is literally someone else's.

Connecting to your Essential Self is the first step in embarking on a new path. I want you to go through the list below and check everything on the list that applies to your life right now.

1. You're stressed, angry, or sad way more often than you feel at peace.
2. Life feels more like a chore than a great adventure.
3. You're seldom in awe.
4. You find solitude uncomfortable.
5. You're bored more often than you're fascinated.
6. You seldom do things you loved doing as a kid.
7. You rarely laugh aloud.
8. You daydream about being elsewhere regularly.

Here is where that magic resides. It's in our discovery of which one of these selves is at the wheel of your life that we will uncover and calibrate in order to retrieve some of that lost power, recovering our ability to act and move forward toward our goals, making informed choices that are based on our truest desires and creating a life we love. Reconciling the Essential Self and the Social Self will help you to be more accountable for your actions, pivoting when they do not match your inner truth.

EXPLORE YOUR ESSENTIAL SELF

Get clear enough about what you really want to be doing with your future. This starts right now, with you. Connect with yourself and get to know yourself on a more intimate level than you ever have before. Work together to challenge you to open up – whether it's looking back, deciding what you want RIGHT NOW, or looking ahead, an openness and attitude of discovery is required. After all, if you're selling pussy, or whatever version of personal "gig" economy you're selling, shouldn't you own it first? And how can you own it, if you're not truly in touch with yourself? In the case that you are wanting out, it's still the same.

Here's a list of activities I do to reconnect with Essential Self.

Breathing. Just simply take a breath in and out and repeat until you feel that your shoulders have found their way back down to where they belong! I talk about this in a later chapter in more detail and expand on why this is important.

Identify your core values. Envision a set of beliefs that represent what is important to you. Next, take stock – are your activities in alignment with those values? Do the people you hang out with make you feel safe, comfortable, positive? The things you spend time on, and the people you spend time with, should be compatible with those values.

Next, there are some activities you can do to reconnect with yourself, and get you in a place where you can identify things that you want to keep, enhance, change, or remove from your life:

- Connect with close friends and family
- Write – whether as a creative outlet or as journaling your thoughts
- Go for a walk, sans headphones – soak up ambient sounds and embrace small details
- Head for the hills – get in the car and change your surroundings, even if just for a few hours
- Turn off technology – get lost in yourself for awhile
- Get more sleep – and make better use of the hours you're awake
- Make some simple diet changes – they will leave you feeling more energized
- Meditate – and create space for calmness

PERFECT DAY/RESTART

If you want to make money, give yourself a comfortable life, like the one you have when you decide to leave the club for a few months on a sabbatical to travel and broaden your own horizons.

I invite you to imagine the perfect in your future life – the one where you've resolved everything holding you back, or found out what you want to do. And when I say perfect, I mean to the T! Get yourself comfortable and close your eyes and take a good few deep breaths. When you are ready, I want you to start by engaging your active imagination. This entire exercise is done with your eyes closed.

There you are just waking up for an entire day of perfect – a perfect day, your perfect day.

Now I want you to become aware of where you are when you open your eyes on that perfect day:

What do you see?

What does your view look like?

Is anyone next to you?

What do you smell?

How do you feel?

What does the bed that you are lying in feel like?

What are the sheets made of...what color...what does your perfect bed look like?

What is the temperature?

What time of day is it?

When you get out of bed...where are you going?

Do you have any rituals you like to do upon waking?

What do you do next?

I want you to notice how your feelings and sensations change, as you walk through your day doing exactly what you want. What does it feel like in your body, to know that there are no worries about money, working, relationships, or whatever is expanding in your daily life at this time. Those are all resolved or aligned while you do this exercise – you've found a way to solve them. Whether through huge efforts, or lots of little deliberate steps, it doesn't matter. For this exercise, you've arrived at a place beyond.

How do you feel?

This is a preview of the life you're meant to have. You can have everything you imagine.

This, my love, is your Essential Self's innate wisdom.

Most people make lists, plans, and goals based on accessing their mind for details, order or organization – but what if you looked at how you wanted to feel?

What if you used that to inform you of your future? What would that look like for you?

I just reverse engineer that shit in order to access my true desires and life force. I notice how that vivifies my spirit and energizes my body. What do you sense in your body when you start imagining and thinking on the possibilities about how you want to feel now and in your future?

If you can remember a time when you knew you needed to get things on your list done and you just didn't feel like it or you got so tired, or if you've forgotten the immediacy of some of that shit on that list, but you know that it is so important for X, Y, Z reasons, these are signs that your mind doesn't agree with your gut – your felt sense of what you should be prioritizing. Your selves are at odds, they are not linked up. Your Essential Self and your Social Self don't agree with the tasks at hand.

What if you were clear about where you were headed, and you made the rules on how to get there based on that clarity? I want you to notice what happens when you feel like you own that! Someone with a strong "why" will be able to figure out "what" or "how," because a strong "why" will lead to unimaginable willpower and persistence.

This is how magic happens. I am not trying to blow smoke up your ass and tell you that life will be perfect if you just do this. I am merely inviting you to try these possibilities on, like you would your stage attire.

Knowing your why is some of the most potent info you can have; it will energize you during your most difficult challenges. It will provide the reserve that keeps you making progress when things aren't perfect. It will illuminate that blind spot that most of us miss, when we're tired, confused, angry, or out of alignment.

Imagine tomorrow: a new day. Imagine that you've decided to do things that provide you a similar energy like you had in your perfect day. Re-create the smell in your room, get a new set of sheets, meet a friend at the beach, take Spanish lessons. Imagine that you will make decisions based on how much closer they bring you to your perfect day.

Before your head hits the pillow tonight, and before you start the next chapter, I want you to pick one thing that you'll do different tomorrow – something just for you, something with just that little hint of perfection. Something to build on.

CRUNCHES FOR YOUR MIND

"Waking up to who you are requires letting go of who you imagined yourself to be."
—Alan Watts

Mindfulness work is based on a few key concepts:

- You most likely are living in survival brain state, your low self, and it is auto piloting you into confusion.
- You are not your thoughts. Thank gawd!
- Most of what you think you think is not your thoughts. They were delivered via FedEx from your people – influencers and all.
- Find your breath (It's easy. It's always right there!).
- To become aware of all of this, you have to breathe.
- Breathe knowing you are watching a shit show.

Breathe again and know you are still watching a shit show. fuuuuuck lol.

The thing about mind work is that most people over think it (see what I did there?). That leads to a lot of misunderstandings about what the hell role your mind has in the first place.

Use the statements above to then free form and create other statements, trying to resolve your thoughts into clear and concise information that you can start to understand. You can only quiet your mind after you first get it to slow down so that you can identify what it is telling you.

YOUR BRAIN WORKS IN FEAR

This may sound familiar.

It's a summer morning, and sunlight is spilling through the trees, filled with singing birds. Merchants are putting out their signs, people are crowding the coffee shops, and someone is rinsing off the sidewalk in front of the market. The beat of the waking city matches your own excited pulse as you head to your first day of work at your new job.

Totally out of the blue, a thought flies in unbidden. *Am I sure that this was a good decision? Can I actually do this? What if my employer goes bankrupt? Is this the best career for me? If I get fired, how can I pay rent?*

You started out completely free from fear. The simple, present moment of your walk to work, maybe even enjoying the sun on your skin, the smell in the air, and the beautiful sense of accomplishment walking into a job you just landed vaporized with a few tiny questions.

You have a part of your brain called the *amygdala*; it is two almond-shaped structures placed in each hemisphere of your brain. I have heard so many names for these little amazing structures, from "reptilian brain," "lizard brain," and "pain in the ass" (that's mine) to "survival mind" and "low self." It's part of your limbic system, which is responsible for emotional and motivational processes, as well as your "fight, flight, or freeze" reaction.

In this case, its job is to help you survive no matter what is happening. The problem is that it doesn't just ignite when there is trouble. It triggers when it *perceives* threat and so sometimes you have your lizard brain dominating more nuanced situations that it's really not suited for. I gotta say that it helps to relate to this part of your mind by naming this little beast of burden cause honestly, she just wants the best for you.

You can learn to bypass those habituated behaviors that have hung around, interrupting and interfering with your life. It could be that despite your hard work and soul searching, you haven't had the success you'd have liked in previous efforts to change your path; perhaps you simply expected more success in the path you're on. These are common frustrations, which might seem even **more** frustrating because you know you've got smarts, drive, and a great heart. Take comfort in knowing that everyone suffers from these sabotages, and you have to learn (and unlearn) to navigate your intelligence. Understand that sometimes you'll have to tell it to piss off!

Here are four core truths about how to approach your thoughts. Harnessing these truths will provide you with a perspective that will help you handle your own mental health and ultimately will empower you at the same time.

DEFUSION

Create a new relationship with your thoughts; instead of driving your thought vehicle directly, use your thoughts as information, such as a map or street signs, that provide you with information that you evaluate in combination with other factors, such as intuition, presence of other cars, and so on.

EXPANSION

When undesired or unpleasant thoughts stroll your way, just accept them – there's no need to react or freak the fuck out. Thoughts are often random, dammit.

CONNECTION

Focus on maintaining a presence focused on what is happening *right now*. Your thoughts often look back, forward, not bound by space or time. That's cool. But you can and should focus your thinking at times. They are YOUR thoughts. It's YOUR mind. It needs to work for you, instead of letting IT drive YOU.

SELF-OBSERVATION

Reflecting on your actions, emotions, thoughts, and experiences as if from a distance, almost equivalent to that of a 3rd party. Detach yourself a bit from these systems, and don't let them fight for control of you.

YOU ARE NOT YOUR THOUGHTS

When we are confronted with issues, we think that if we could just think more about them, we will figure out the solutions. We clear time to do more thinking. When we try to understand why we are feeling the way we do, or why we are acting or reacting the way we do, guess where we often go? More thinking! Concentrate. Focus. Figure it out. We make strained attempts to look into our memories to locate info about the current crisis or discomfort, to see if that will inform us. Maybe that will unlock our blind spot and all of a sudden all will be revealed! People often make assumptions about who they are based on thoughts that either were learned by unreliable sources, or came from concepts that they aren't really connected to.

What if I told you that most of what you think about is based solely on the dead corpses of other people's words, statements, and thoughts? Most of what you think you think are not *your* thoughts; they were handed down from generations before you, from your people, your culture, and your environment. They are regurgitated beliefs based on unproven concepts that other people came up with in their search for the meaning in their life. What's that got to do with you?

How can you realize your future goals, if you're not clear about how you think? You have to know how you know!

This is what I know about my thoughts from all the work I put into healing from my childhood/young adulthood abuse. The series of stories I had about what had happened in my childhood that I thought were all true were actually keeping me from healing. It didn't matter how hard I worked. I realized slowly, over time, that what I understood about what happened came to me from outside my awareness, and it was my memories, and my thoughts about those memories, that held me captive in misery and despair.

Much of the time our memories are really not an accurate way of "keeping score," and more times than not, they set us up for trouble. They create limited beliefs, setting you up for victimization later. This is a great opportunity to engage your observer and navigate your memories with that perspective.

Understanding that your mind can be both imperfect and inaccurate was a very important distinction for me to make, because I just knew that I was somehow sabotaging my success and healing.

It was part of my life script! It was a complimentary gift all for me, and it came from the family and environment I was birthed into. Learning that allowed me to own what happened next. It was actual control, rather than perceived control, which no one could ever take from me.

You are running on life scripts. Can you recall memories or experiences in your relationships where you felt that you were a character in a movie not of your choosing? Your thinking doesn't inform your decisions, and it's a real waste of time to stay stuck in your mind frantically searching for how to change your life. Cognitive rumination is a power guzzler.

Add to this mindfuck fest that your thoughts are directly related to your suffering. Thoughts are almost useless in making life-transforming decisions. So what's the key to making lasting transformative changes? Realizing that beliefs generate thoughts. Those are the true informers of your success, or lack thereof.

We often become what we believe ourselves to be. What if the following quote were true:

"What the mind can conceive and believe, it can achieve."
– Napolean Hill

Who would you be, if this were true for you? How different would you be? How different would your life be right now if this were true for you?

"Man often becomes what he believes himself to be. If I keep on saying to myself that I cannot do a certain thing, it is possible that I may end by really becoming incapable of doing it. On the contrary, if I have the belief that I can do it, I shall surely acquire the capacity to do it even if I may not have it at the beginning."
– Mahatma Gandhi

You have to focus on your beliefs to get some traction on making powerful transformative changes. It's your beliefs, body, and emotions that inform your decisions and create personal empowerment. The information that already exists in you creates long-lasting changes for your life and your future. You can have anything you desire if you tap into your already existing wisdom.

Now, let's take a look at your beliefs.

Ask yourself:

- When did I start believing?
- Who taught me the above belief?

- Can you remember a time when you questioned these first two thoughts?

Now, let's have a look at how attached you are to those thoughts:

- What would it mean if I changed my mind on this issue?
- Who would be affected by my changing mind?
- What happened for you? It might have been some version of WTF, or flooding thoughts about getting this right.

Bring your awareness to your feelings. What did you feel when you answered the above questions.

Notice what happens when I say the following statement: You are not your thoughts, you are *having* thoughts.

Give yourself a few minutes, however much time you need, to watch your mind search.

If you are *having* the thought, then who would you be *without* that thought?

This process can be a myth buster in your daily life and will help you get in touch with what matters for you. This simple concept can create a good amount of cognitive dissonance, or personal discord (incongruence) when it comes to your experience versus reality.

It might seem pretty complicated, but if you were to just concentrate on the above questions, you will have a great place to start realizing that a lot of your power goes down the tube from "thinking."

If you are confused, that's OK. Stay calm. It may not be clear now, but it becomes clear as you move toward the person you are becoming. It's some of the magic I have spoken about earlier. Not knowing what you are thinking is a way of keeping you out of the driver's seat of your life. It is taking away from your inherent right to know and experience completely.

How can you realize your future goals if you are not clear about how you think?

You have to know *how* you know. If you don't know how you think, how do you change your life in the way that you want?

If you want more money, a better man, a better house, a better club to work in, or a better future than your parents or the people down the block – where would you start? Would you even trust that these are your wants?

SO HOW SHOULD YOU USE YOUR MIND, THEN?

Your mind is like a herd of wild stallions. It will take you for the ride of your life, over and over and over again. The point is to cultivate enough awareness so that you own the reins of your mind, and in the process creating you as the *observer*. And poof! Consciousness, or your awareness, is born!

So what do you do with your thoughts? You relax. You let them flow. You remember that they don't define you. You become the observer, letting your thoughts fill the roles of analyst, processor, idea generator. Your mind is an amazing asset. It's an *engine*, not the driver. Give it some gas, change gears, idle at a stop light. Sometimes it needs to just get out of your way. Your mind is only an engine. *You're* the driver.

When you become the observer, you are able to take a step back from your mind and witness what is going on without trying to change it. It's still you in there, but there is some separation, some safety, some perspective. Have you ever seen a friend or loved one struggle with a problem when the solution seemed clear and obvious to you? That's the power of the observer.

Becoming the observer, using this information, instead of letting it drive you, will allow you to sustain focus on, isolate, and remove the damage caused by overthinking, and let all your systems have balanced input. You will be more aligned and consistent in your decision-making.

The Samurai swordsman Miyamoto Musashi stressed the difference between perceiving and observing. The perceiving eye is weak, he wrote, but the observing eye is strong. Why?

Because strategy – whether in business or winning sword fights– requires objectivity and seeing things as they are. It requires us to put aside the emotions that cloud our thinking with fear or brimming overconfidence and see how the situation truly is.

Consider how knowing this plays into your life as a stripper/dancer. How would being the observer help you earn more money? Or execute on goals that you are working toward?

You might like to visualize your thoughts as pictures projected up onto a movie screen, while your awareness is "you" sitting in the audience watching the show. Or you might like to picture your thoughts as clouds that drift across the sky of your awareness.

Labeling is another useful technique. This is especially helpful when you are doing a breath meditation or body scan and you become involved in a stream of consciousness, a thought stream, which is a distraction from your chosen object of awareness.

When you eventually catch yourself having drifted away, you might note that fact using the label "thinking" and say that to yourself before gently escorting your attention back to the breath or body.

Another realization and question you may be asking yourself right now is, "If I'm not my thoughts (because I am able to observe them) then who am I? Who is observing?"

You may see that you are not your thoughts, and you are in control of how you act in response to them. You may see that maybe, just maybe, life is more about removing the layers within than adding layers on top, which may bring you to the discovery that you possess everything you need to live a full and rich life.

Discovering the power of your spirit, and seeing your limitations dissolve through this inner work, is the real adventure. It's knowing that this incredible being was here all-along, and peeling off the layers that shrouded her. This is your intended journey.

I would be naive to sit here and give you an answer to who the observer is, but searching for that answer yourself may reveal that, in fact, you are stronger and more resilient than you ever imagined.

The realization that you are not your thoughts, that your thoughts, added up, do not compose you, allows you to change your perspective. This distance allows you to be more forgiving and tolerant of the thoughts you do have. You can notice the occasions when they bring you answers and laugh knowingly at the times when your fear or ego get carried away. This is some Jedi mind shit right here!

I couldn't possibly give you all the information needed to map a life course of thinking in this one book. I believe there are numerous layers and levels to our thinking. I'd like to illustrate how you can empower yourself with your thinking. I'll show you how an unempowered thought can simply be replaced by an empowering one. You will always want to choose the freedom of the empowered thought over the limitations of the unempowered one.

Let's start with an unempowered version of you. You might ask yourself, "Why do I always get picked last?" You might mean it sarcastically, but your sneaky mind will try to answer that query. It will start trying to come up with answers, making them up: you're not good enough, too slow, or not very bright.

Here's how the empowered version of you will sound: "What can I learn from this?" or "I'm going to get the most out of this that I can." Thinking this way will not only make you feel better in the moment but also set you up for a more positive experience and provide an opportunity for growth.

When I was contemplating a career as a midwife, I found that I was plagued by a lot of competing, negative, and limiting beliefs in my mind. I noticed that I struggled whether to even research the possibilities.

When I want to change directions in my life or when I am pivoting, I like to contemplate and imagine, in addition to researching possibilities. It's the way I start to create my life. It's my version of magic. Building a house starts with a foundation before adding the walls, windows, and doors. For a long time, I was having trouble constructing that foundation, so I would get stuck.

I say stuck, but I'm confrontational, even with myself. Respectfully disruptive is one way I like to characterize it. So I persisted, trying to unblock myself, eventually engaging a therapist to help address these blocks.

In one particular session, she asked me to get out a piece of paper and draw a line down the middle. On the right side, I was instructed to add a potent negative belief that I believed was preventing me from accomplishing my goal. On the left side, I needed to add a thought that I wanted to believe, a thought that would directly lead to accomplishing my goal.

Next, I started having a conversation between the negative belief and the positive one. As the conversation evolved, the only rule was that the positive belief stayed constant throughout.

I would start with the negative belief and reply with the unchanging positive belief. After each positive belief statement, I'd pause and let my negative belief voice evolve and respond, repeating the process until the negative beliefs had a chance to air their dirty laundry and eventually ran out of excuses for the juggernaut that I let my positive belief be in this moment.

Positive Belief	Negative Belief
"You can learn new material."	"I'm not smart enough to learn all this midwife stuff."
"You can learn new material."	"I don't think I can do it."
"You can learn new material."	"I'm too judgmental."
"You can learn new material."	"What if I get sick?"
"You can learn new material."	"It's too hard!"
"You can learn new material."	"I'm scared."
"You can learn new material."	"Maybe."
"You can learn new material."	"It's too hard."
"You can learn new material."	"With help."
"You can learn new material."	"With patience."
"You can learn new material."	"OK"

I was absolutely stunned as I saw what felt like two attorneys arguing their cases on my behalf. The magic of this exercise is that it allowed me to see just how empowered I can be when I give myself the authority to challenge these doubts, whether their source is from the dark parts of my soul or learned excuses from my environment.

This exercise was, and continues to this day, to be a very powerful and transformational tool to get unstuck. I can do it in my head, on the spot, wherever I am.

There are two primary goals of this exercise:

1. Identify the paralyzing fears that are blocking you from accomplishing your goals, and

2. Deliver the message to yourself that your positive beliefs are boss-level and that they aren't going away or letting those doubts and fears rule the roost any more.

The key to this exercise is realizing that it totally depends on your secret code to unlock its power. It has to be your voice – both the positive one and the negative one. You have to allow the negative one to answer, just as you have to marshal the strength when you summon your positive belief.

Now it's your turn to experience some of that magic for yourself. Go grab some paper and a pen or whatever.

Draw a line right down the center of the paper. On the right side on the top of the page I want you to write down the negative belief you believe is in your way and won't let you have what you want.

On the left side, I want you to write down what you would rather believe. Then go back to the other side of the page and inquire into yourself again what the negative belief is that is keeping you from what you want. Sometimes it will be the same belief, sometimes not. It takes patience. Give it to yourself. Go back and forth; you will notice it slowly changing, as it does in the table above. It will slowly transform as you contemplate the belief you would rather have.

And now, you breathe.

MEDITATION FOR HIDDEN DRAGONS

One of the biggest obstacles I have heard from clients in the past is that meditation is "too hard," but after they realized what meditation really is, they started a journey that helped them unlock and order their thoughts and place them in the proper context. Shit just started to make sense. So much sense. And they were able to react to the daily triggers in a different and surprising way.

You will have to find your **breath**. It's easy. It's always right there!

You can do all the thinking you want. It falls short, however, when it comes to answering the big questions about your life's biggest dilemmas. I want to invite you to move your thoughts to the side and see what more there is for you to discover. Once you have enough of a clear experience you will reach the conclusion that breathing is far more helpful than thinking your way through to the other side of transformation. With breath, you can increase your capacity to tolerate confusion. Which is fucking great when you are going through any breakdown in life, until you make it to the breakthrough.

There is a beginning, middle, and end to one single breath. It's simple. You got this. Now, I want you to do it. Close your eyes, and bring your awareness to your breathing. Notice how shallow or fast you are breathing and let it happen. No force necessary. Now bring your awareness to the next breath, and notice on inhalation, the "beginning." Next notice the "middle," and when you are pushing air out of your mouth, you will notice the "end." Now repeat as many times as you can. When you find your attention focused elsewhere – no need to get crazy ass hard on yourself – simply bring your awareness back to breathe: beginning, middle, and end.

Life is meant to be danced, not thought. Dancing into your own body is what your breath does for you. The benefits are so numerous that every human knows and enjoys a connection to that awareness – that observer that lives within each of us. It is a primary source of peace and equanimity, it helps reduce stress, and most of all it helps you resolve what you "think" you need to be doing, what you should be feeling, or what you should be giving of yourself. In time, it will start to whisper back to you your unique wisdom, organically revealing what it is you were seeking. Learning the skill of surrender is tremendously powerful and will support you along your path to empowerment. It can also help when dealing with shame, with tortured thoughts about who you must be if you are dancing naked for money.

For the most part, what you think has nothing to do with why you are feeling like shit. You are feeling like shit because you have some limited beliefs that are creating emotions that cycle through like a Ferris wheel. And you are most likely attempting to control your thoughts and emotions with little to no success. What's funnier is that you are probably doing it over and over and over again expecting different results. Insanity! You're not alone.

No one wants to feel like shit. That's why this society has successfully created really good distractions. Like drinking, and sex, and shopping, and crazy reality shows where the people seem to have way more fucked up lives than ours, we think – Ha! Please.

Let's get something straight, sister, you cannot control your thoughts or emotions. Your reactions and your choices, sure. Get ready, cause right here, sis, is where I ask you for that truth-telling bravery with yourself.

You will need to drop the act. You need something called psychological flexibility. That's the shit, and it is lit, real lit! Trust me, the more psychological flexibility – the super skill of your mental health – you have, the more you are in the driver's seat of your vehicle and not in the back seat somewhere.

Psychological flexibility will allow you to maintain a more even-keeled, long-term perspective – it will allow you room to let your thoughts and emotions ping-pong all over the place, without necessarily having to act on them. Again, placing yourself as the observer will be super helpful in maximizing your psychological flexibility. You'll use your thoughts and emotions as information, helping you understand yourself, and your environment – without giving them total control.

This is extremely valuable, since thoughts and emotions often oscillate pretty dramatically, often in a short time. Isolating them will give you a powerful buffer, providing more stability and consistency as you navigate relationships, challenges, and situations that arise in your day-to-day life.

FEELINGS IN THOUGHT

A major part of making transformational changes in your life is exploring how you want to feel versus what you think you should be wanting or doing in order to make major money, or at least enough money to get by, or have a great man or an amazing career with meaning or whatever – fill in the blank.

One of the clearest ways that I know about how to access that desired state is through sitting down with my Essential Self and having an open and fucking raw convo with her. She knows all that wisdom shit!

You just want to be able to get out of your way, so that you can make the changes you need to leave the shame and guilt behind and level up.

I don't want to leave out your Social Self, seeing as she is the one who throws down! She has a major stake in your game and you are gonna want her in your corner to pull on all her perspective.

We all want to feel like we belong, we matter, we all have a primal need to be seen, heard, and, most of all, accepted unconditionally. These are primal needs that exist for the actualizing. These are all governed by your girl, the Social Self.

Your thoughts hold you captive within an endless cycle of suffering, and if you are unable to create a friendly witness, you will continue in immobility in your life. We are human; therefore, we suffer. To be human is to suffer, but how? And why? In searching for answers to these existential life questions, we can find our way, our unique blueprint and our access to true joy.

There's some intentionally mind-blowing content in this chapter, designed to help you reset and rewire the way you think and the way you use your thoughts. I have some videos and other bonus content that will be great companion tools to help you understand and reinforce these ideas and processes on my website at http://angelinalombardo.com/love-letters/resources.

YOUR BODY = GENIUS

"The body has a way of remembering everything the mind deletes. There will be no erasing of me."

—Eron Van Vuren

THE CHAIR

Throughout my life I have seen many therapists. I saw some specifically for sexual abuse. I was open to just about any style or modality of therapy if I believed it would help me clear the confusion in my life with picking assholes as lovers. Here's a little story about an encounter I had with a therapist a very long time ago:

I remember that when I entered the room where our session was going to take place, I noticed that she had her chair and my chair separated by a chasm of empty space. I was like, "Well, maybe she needs all that space 'cause she doesn't really like the clients she works with." The session started by her directing me to "feel with my body" into the space of the room, the space between her, the chairs, and me.

We started by standing extremely close together – almost touching – and she instructed me to pay attention to the sensations that I noticed in my body and to answer based on my perceptions of what I was feeling. She would ask, "How do you feel about the amount of space between us?" I would answer, "There's not enough," gauging from how tense my muscles felt. After each response, I took a step back. Little bit by little bit, it was clear to me that there was a lot of information, right there in my body! I was surprised how much room I really needed at that time to truly feel comfortable. My mind and body had very different ideas of how much distance I needed.

My body was speaking to me through my tense muscles and was revealing to me how tense I felt around people. It also showed me that I knew when I was uncomfortable or comfortable, which was not very often, with someone. For the most part I was walking around extremely uncomfortable with everyone! Once I learned to listen to my body's helpful information, not only did I get better at figuring out how to keep myself from feeling uncomfortable, but it also started to inform my healing process.

Unbeknownst to me, I had been living my life up to that point reacting to my environment from an unembodied state, due to the abuse I had suffered in my past. This made sense to me.

From the unembodied perspective, while I was being abused, I just fucking up and left! I couldn't stay safely in that environment, so I jumped out of my body and watched from outside. Sometimes, I didn't even stay to watch. I just straight up had "places" I would go where it was blank space in order to survive my abuse.

Up to this point, I hadn't given myself permission to show up in my life for myself. How the hell could I? I just thought there was something wrong with me, because I was broken from abuse. I knew that if I could find it, I would repair it – simple, maybe, but definitely not easy.

I had to learn how to climb back into my body, to peer into what I had stored up in there. It was a fucking nightmare, but everything about it amazed me, truly amazed me. I worked with many practitioners on my unembodied state. The reflection I want to speak about here comes from my reading of a very special book titled *Waking the Tiger* by Peter Levine.

In my case, I had been traumatized from a very early age. My Essential Self experienced acute stress from a perceived life-threat. When we experience traumatic events, such as with my abuse or when you're driving and see a cat dart in front of your car, science has shown that a physiological response occurs: your body tenses, your breathing quickens, you clench your fists until your knuckles turn white. Your body experiences stress. This response is the body's instinctual "fight, flight, or freeze" response. A cascade of chemicals is released in our body as it prepares to survive the perceived threat. This is the physiological wisdom of our body.

INTEROCEPTION: OUR SENSES AND EMOTIONS

Our emotions are deeply and directly connected to our physical bodies. When the tall person behind you on the plane puts their knees into you, when you get the wrong pizza, when someone cuts in line, your body will unconsciously get ready for battle. You might feel flush with silent rage and tense with readiness and experience a raciness in your pulse. Still, you're civilized, so it might take you a moment to even realize that you're angry; your body got there first. Interoception is your awareness of these signs. Interoception's role is extremely important in helping us realize and figure out our emotions. As we become more aware and experienced in interpreting the shades and hues of our emotions, we also can identify it in others.

Humans really have eight senses. The way we understand the world is mediated by our five senses: touch, taste, sound, smell, and sight. The other three are vestibular, proprioception, and interoception. Vestibular is concerned with balance. Proprioception is the sense of the relative position of one's own parts of the body and strength of effort being employed in movement. Interoception is the sense that helps you understand and feel what's going on inside your body.

Not only does interoception allow you to feel your heart racing, squeamishness, or shortness of breath, but it is also closely linked to your sense of self-identity and similarly connected to your Essential Self. Your interoception sense integrates and communicates these sensations. For these reasons, interoception is a strong ally in feeling and understanding your emotions and maintaining a healthy channel of information. For example, if your sense of interoception is underdeveloped or blocked, you might have latent, volcanic emotional reactions.

Let's make this simple. Have you caught that Snickers commercial on TV? It introduces the concept of being "hangry." Picture Betty White playing football with a boatload of young men. She keeps getting tackled – clearly not very elusive – as you'd expect from the agility of a ninety-six-year-old (still gorgeous) actress. Finally, the guys ask her what her deal is. She responds, "Come on, you guys have been riding me all day." A young woman enters the frame. "Babe," she calls, and hands Betty White a Snickers bar. Betty chomps it down and immediately transforms into a young man. The announcer says, "You're not yourself when you're hungry." This is a classic example of how this sense can inform you.

BODY SMARTS

The body knows. Our culture often tells us to ignore our bodies – push through the tiredness, ignore the pain, fight the fatigue, don't let anyone see your nervousness. The body, if we allow it and learn how to listen to it, gives us information. It's most aligned with our Essential Self. It's one language our Essential Self uses to get our attention.

In fact, if we use our mind to suppress our body's channel of information, in some people your body will respond with louder, stronger signals to try to get your attention. This may even manifest itself in stress or sickness.

Unlike your sneaky ass mind, however, your body has a special power: it can't lie. It won't lie. This is why it's so fucking valuable as a trusted advisor. It's not just that it's cleverer than your mind; it's that it's so much wiser and always accurate.

I had a client who had begun experiencing stomach pain every morning in his office after breakfast. Initially convinced it was diet-related, he tried switching up what he ate to try to find out if he had food sensitivities. After failing to find anything conclusive, he sought out the advice of his doctor. Shortly before scheduling a barrage of invasive gastrointestinal tests at the request of his primary physician, he mentioned this pain on a call. I asked him to walk me through his morning routine. Eventually, we found out that he started experiencing this pain shortly after being asked to "fudge the numbers" for a new morning report to his regional VP. Your body's looking out for you; it's not easily fooled and won't shut up, even if you ask it to.

THE POWER IN YOUR BODY

I have paid dearly to have the knowledge and awareness that I have. It was raw, unadulterated abuse or self-victimization at times but pure bliss and magic self-love at others. I have weaved in and out of the lanes when it comes to cultivating a relationship with my body, goddess temple that it is, a miracle of alchemical transformative wisdom.

And then, it broke. For good, I thought. It was doing things without considering me at all. It was leading me into some pretty terrifying times. I was going down hard. First it was just fatigue; then it turned into raging moons (periods) that were out of control, heavy bleeding, and then came the hallucinating migraines. Next came the panic attacks, and the nauseating upset tummy. Then my body became fragile and withered. I could not keep weight on, to – pardon the pun – save my life.

All of this was happening while I was working sixteen to seventeen hours a day to keep my daughter, remain self-sufficient with a roof over our heads, and keep food in our mouths.

I had just had her returned to me, so quitting was not an option. I had no idea what was happening inside of me. It had been shortly after my first experience with ayahuasca– a plant medicine used in spiritual ceremonies – with a shaman from Peru. I had theorized that my physiological breakdown might be my body's wise ways of trying to regain balance. I thought it was a sort of putting back together, but in a different way.

I had a complete breakdown. I had put so many concepts around self-healing inside. In an effort to heal myself, I just kept stuffing them in. I tried to tell myself that I was getting closer, and I knew that I was. Still, I was blocked. There were big shifts and mini breakdowns and occasionally huge breakthroughs. But something was just off the entire time.

There is so much to be gained by listening to and learning about the language of the body. Its power is so much more than making lazy men feel desired and attractive. It can break, and the thing is, you can heal yourself if you know how. It contains everything you have been through, good and bad, traumatizing and liberating. It is a system unto itself, and for you not to understand it is cheating you of some of the most potent power there is in being human.

Before my body broke, I had been invited by a close friend to my first ayahuasca ceremony.

I was thirty-one. It blew my mind wide open and dissolved all the beliefs I had crafted up to that point.

I was also able to viscerally feel and see, with such a deep wisdom, the energetic weight that my body was carrying around on a daily basis. In that one ceremony, I felt how heavy it was physically. It was so heavy, in fact, that I started having an extremely hard time breathing. I had the intense sensation that something was crushing me. It was the weight from all of my accumulated trauma and stored emotions by way of denial. I started to become increasingly cognizant of its presence on my back, and oh my gawd, that shit was a revelation to view and viscerally experience. It gifted me with perspective.

So much more was experienced, but the most important message I learned is that there is a wealth of information right inside the mystery and miracle that is your body.

The *ayahuasquero* who was guiding the ceremony shared one very clear message with me during our time together: "You don't have roots; you have no ground." I initially took that to mean I wasn't a calm person energetically or that I appeared erratic. In retrospect, it became clear that he meant that I was without, because I clearly was not wholly grounded within. I was bypassing the physical experiences in my life. Basically, I was in body denial. I was busy "thinking" my way through my healing without using my experiential knowledge as a whole.

I had to surrender into the darkness of illness and the scary aspects of being out of control of my body, no matter how hard I tried to use, access, and solve with my mind, to free myself.

I have always been a deeply spiritual person and turned to these values to guide me through my experiences moving forward in my healing.

"Healing depends on experiential knowledge. You can be fully in charge of your life only if you can acknowledge the reality of your body, in all its visceral dimensions."
– *Elvin Semrad*

ENERGY

Emotions can also become stuck in your body. Your entire body works, is alive, is an animated, autonomous entity, thanks to energy. It's not just a mystical experience, left to the people who "believe." Life force energy simply means that there is an energy force running through you. On a very basic level, life energy is the energy that is present in living things and absent from nonliving things. Bodily functions occur because life energy drives those processes, not because of interactions between the chemicals that compose it.

The study of quantum physics has proven that everything in the universe is made of pure energy; everything is made up of large groups of subatomic particles that differ only in characteristics such as rate of vibration. Scientists have proven beyond doubt that the physical world is one large sea of energy that flashes in and out of being in a fraction of a second, over and over again. Nothing is solid; everything is made up of nonphysical energy that can be physically directed to create what we desire.

This is important, because while we often study, classify, and experiment on things that we perceive as static – everything, even the most dense, solid, immovable matter – is comprised of energy. Quantum physics is calling our attention to the awareness that energy that forms the subatomic particles that comprise EVERY atom, in every molecule, in every cell, in every body. We are one big mass of energy – we are energy beings.

There is a "no bullshit" clause in my makeup. I'm sharing this shit because it makes common sense. It's profound and important to know how large a role energy has in our lives.

There is also an experience of a phenomenon called mystical energy. Mystical energy is what you sense when you are inspired. You are inspired as you feel the absence of blockage, negation, worry, shyness, anger, and stress, and you are functioning at a level much higher than before." In her book, *SuperMind: The Ultimate Energy*, Barbara Brown calls this the "higher-functioning mind." After you start to feel mystical energy, you often perform tasks that you couldn't perform before. You may be surprised that you are performing these tasks. You feel that you are being guided by a higher intelligence or power.

Having a sense of your body's energy, it's sources, and how they affect you will continually serve you as you seek to feel, and then understand, what it is trying to tell you. This information source is at least as important as the nearly nonstop activity of the mind, and certainly will be a more consistent companion for collaboration. It will be with you every step of the way as you make choices and start navigating toward outcomes that work for you.

7

#WTFFEELINGDECODERRINGACTIVATE

"Be who you needed when you were younger."

—Unknown

One of the many benefits of learning about feeling into your body is that you can learn to better understand and get in touch with your emotions. Emotions are often categorized as mystical, ethereal, and elusive, so maybe defining them would be great place to start. Many people get feelings and emotions confused with each other:

An emotion is a physiological experience (or state of awareness) in your body, that gives you information about the world.

A feeling is your conscious awareness, and mental processing, of the emotion itself.

Some people get this distinction naturally. This might be new to you, and even if you were aware of these concepts, you might not have been experiencing feelings and emotions this way. As you might expect, since you're getting to know me a lil' bit, I'm going to tell you that this is fine and perfectly normal!

Humans suffer greatly from emotional constipation. No book, system, ideology, or person should ever be allowed to supplant your own wisdom. Instead learn and then trust that your emotions are tools of your deepest awareness. This entry will be a natural progression, allowing your emotions the trust to take you on the journey they gift you.

Your emotions are a significant part of your being. They are the force that shapes your day, dictating exactly how you will be proceeding, from the moment you wake up until the second your head hits the pillow. You might as well get cozy with feeling, because it doesn't stop happening until you die (or so you might think – but that's another conversation than the one I am starting here!).

UNDERSTAND YOUR EMOTIONS – DON'T BLOCK THEM!

There's a lot of misinformation about emotions and where to put them. For too long, emotions have been associated with instability, immaturity, and an inability to stay grounded in reality. Though there's been a shift in some cultures to accept and embrace emotions, they still are often regarded as something to repress, redirect, or brush off – only to be dealt with when there's no other option. Emotion means "drama;" emotional people are "dramatic," and emotions are still associated with being or acting irrationally.

Even if you feel differently, there's so much conditioning, from our friends and other relationships, that dictate how freely we can exchange, express, and experience our emotions in a comfortable and supported way.

Sometimes, emotions are only experienced in outbursts, likely because we are trained to suppress them, and so after being neglected, they make themselves known in any way that they can. People who are both supported in experiencing their emotions and have an understanding of them are actually less prone to outburst, because they are regularly in touch with those emotions, and know what they are telling them, leaving these outbursts unnecessary.

Through feeling into your body, and supporting and nurturing your understanding of emotions, you will receive so much more helpful information that will guide you and reassure you. You will look forward to the information you receive from them, much as you would appreciate a construction sign telling you the bridge up ahead is closed for repairs.

Life is meant to be danced, not thought about, divorced from the moment-by-moment experience. Feelings are meant to be danced not analyzed. Feel into them, let them inform you.

CONFUSION, IN EFFECT

Here's an example of emotions in action. I will use some of what I have learned on my path, as well as concepts I've learned from my spirit animal, Karla McLaren.

One of my biggest issues in life was, and still is, confusion. Although I have a different way of understanding and approaching it now, moving forward, it is still my default. If I am overwhelmed, I am confused. When I feel pressure, I am confused. When I need to make big life decisions, I claim that I can't and blame confusion. It's my great cop-out in the sky. I used to think there was something seriously wrong with me.

I didn't understand that confusion was my warning sign that the bridge was out up ahead, that I needed to find a detour from my current direction. Confusion doesn't really dig when you try to work around it. It's like that asshole you knew in high school who blocks your way in the skinny hallway, and when you try to go around, he slides right back in front of you. What a dick. Of course, there are many ways to deal with that asshole. Ignore him? Might work. Run around and go the long way? Late for class or, worse, he follows you. Confront him? Right hook? He was hoping for that.

Confusion will often zap your focus, even if you try to go in a totally different direction. You're lost, the nervousness drains your energy. It's hard to function, because confusion is fucking with you, especially in those ways in which you need to get clarity, make decisions, and move forward. The more you try to think about it, the worse your thinking gets.

Confusion is definitely that asshole. But confusion is also a gift, like that "Bridge Out Ahead" sign. It's your body letting you know that something is not aligned, that you're about to make a bad decision, or that it's not comfortable with the situation. It's actually protecting you in the form of attention-grabbing inconvenience.

Trust your body. Trust the gift that is confusion. Accept that it's telling you something, and stop trying to go around it or go through it. Take a step back, and try to figure out why it's there. Peel back the layers that got you here, and you'll find that it will stop fighting you. Look at the other tendrils of thoughts around you, and you'll find what's been distracting you. Appreciate that confusion is doing its best to prevent you from fucking up. He might always be an asshole, but he's got your best interests at heart. And by the way, you're late for work.

PUTTING IT INTO PRACTICE

I learned all of that from Karla McLaren's book *The Language of Emotions.* For me, I really identified with the concept of my "survival mode" being stuck on overdrive! I was doing a whole shit ton of reacting, without any patience to take stock of the events in my life. I was just reacting, reacting, reacting, without any thought. I *did* believe I was considering my circumstance and inevitable consequences, but I was so ill-informed. Emotions get their power from a simple but deep-seated source: our lack of self-knowledge. I was repeating self-defeating emotional responses over and over without relief.

I've since figured out how to break this pattern, and put into place new ones that honor my needs as well as the needs of others. I'm excited to share my insights and support you in your growth.

What would it be like for you to feel free from the suffering that your emotions seem to stimulate? What would it be like for you to be emotionally balanced?

We all go through stages of emotional experience. Here are three primary stages of emotional maturity that will help you understand the way you interact with your emotions, as well as understand the different ways that others interact with their emotions.

In Stage 1, we are concerned for other people's feelings. We feel angry or upset if we think they have done something that triggers our feelings. We make compromises in the hopes that we'll increase the happiness of others. We get down, or even feel responsible, when those we care about are unhappy.

Stage 2 is about focusing on our own feelings and ensuring that our own happiness is not compromised. This is a reaction and progression from the sense that we've been overly focused on the feelings of others. Our own feelings, compromised in Stage 1, are given more priority, sometimes even to the point where we don't seem too concerned with the feelings of others. This stage might be seen as selfish or self-absorbed.

Stage 3 is a natural combination of the first two stages. We understand that both our feelings, and the feelings of others, are important. We have an awareness that we are responsible for our own feelings, and that we are able to notice when our actions affect others. This ability to value the emotions of others, without taking responsibility for them, is also called emotional liberation. We are able to freely share our emotions, and support and respect the emotions of others, understanding their value and necessary role in our lives.

You probably won't be surprised to learn that your Social Self governs Stage 1 and Stage 2 and that Stage 3 is much more aligned with your Essential Self.

EMOTIONAL REACTIVITY

Growing up, I was told to be seen and not heard. What a contradiction. When I was "seen" it was typically under assumptive circumstances. If I looked distressed or upset by something I was being told, I would get a backhand or a punch to the face. For a while, it was a regular occurrence that my mother, who would literally seem to fly through the air toward me in a split second and grip my neck, nails digging into my flesh, lifting me off the ground, would be spitting and spouting her impassioned message into my face about hiding my emotions.

Since I had become conditioned at an early age to suppress my emotional reactions, my emotional ineptness was fertile ground for the exhausting rollercoaster ride that is emotional reactivity once I was on my own. Emotions will take us to blissful peak states, the depths of delusion and despair, and everything in between.

In my memory there are many incidents where I had had trouble denoting the difference between my emotional experience, contrasted with what others were saying to me about their experience. We have all been in relationships where we have had disagreements with what our partners were saying about their perceived truth compared with what we thought was happening. It might start from a simple statement like, "If you could just be more caring, then I wouldn't be so rigid, and we would get along better." Statements like these can easily spiral into a cycle of triggered responses; you might withdraw into negative self-talk, or perhaps get angry, and blame the other person, and respond harshly. Either way, the response to an emotional discussion will have a negative association and only cause you more problems in the future.

As you can see, my ladies, emotional reactivity is one of the major causes of disempowerment. You can NOT afford to give away your energy to empty spaces and that is literally what happens when you choose to react rather than "hold" the tension of your emotions. It takes courage, commitment, and self-awareness, but it's definitely possible to release your emotional patterns. You can create new patterns that allow you to consider your feelings without reacting. You can learn to leverage this emotional liberation to avoid regrettable conflicts and make choices that reflect your true needs, keeping your Social Self from dominating the conversation.

Let's use an example from your life. Grab a piece a paper and write down a known emotional trigger of your own. You can choose one from your past or one that you currently have now. Write it out. In fact, I want you to be as detailed as you can be.

As you are writing this out, I want you to be aware of what is taking place emotionally for you as you write. There's no need to write this down. Just notice.

Next, I want you to become the observer. Don't judge these emotions as you experience them, and don't judge yourself for having them. They aren't good or bad. They are just information. Once you're more experienced and comfortable with noticing and evaluating your emotional information, you'll find yourself making better decisions, you'll find yourself making more progress in making profound changes in your life, and you'll see greater progress in your process.

Here is another approach. Refrain from acting out in words or action. This allows you to deescalate an emotional response, effectively interrupting the storyline. When you are in conflict with someone else, put this practice into play.

You will notice that if you act out through thoughts, words, and actions such as arguing, screaming, hitting, or blaming (yourself or another person), you'll never get in touch with the underlying feeling responsible for your pain. And so, you'll never be able to heal the original wound.

You may truly believe that someone else has caused your emotions because our stories can be so strong, so convincing.

Here is another example of what happens when you are emotionally triggered.

Imagine a dog on a master's leash. The neighborhood tom cat strolls into the scene. Suddenly, the master is struggling to hold on to the leash as the dog lurches, barking loudly, intent on catching the cat who's tripping car alarms, jumping from hood to hood down the street.

It's very normal to react naturally to the sounds, words, and experiences in our environment with responses that might not reflect our true intentions, feelings, or values. The dog is just like an emotionally reactive person, chasing cats and barking at the doorbell instinctively and incessantly. However, with focus and practice, each of us can become a master, choosing which cats to chase and which to let stroll by. Learning this discipline isn't easy, but it is certainly valuable. It also doesn't prevent you from chasing cats, if that's ultimately what you decide to do.

COURAGE AND FEELING

Courage is not an empty word. It is a feeling state, and it needs exercising. We can look at emotions as muscles as well, which need to be used and nurtured in order for them to guide you back to your inner authentic nature. Courage is what it takes to keep on your path with this practice.

This is where we find peace, and a soft quiet place to rejuvenate enough to go back into the world of contact. In feeling your feelings, there is a release.

I approach the sometimes challenging work of feeling my emotions by bringing my awareness to the sensations in my body, as I listen for the conversation with whatever arises. I start by breathing and watching.

How do you approach your emotions? How often do you bring your awareness to your emotions throughout the day? If you do it at all, what do you notice?

Do you notice how you see yourself for feeling your emotions? What are some of the phrases or sentences you hear yourself saying?

What sensations do you notice in your body when you resist what you're feeling?

Have you ever noticed how exhausted you feel, trying not to feel?

I know emotions as destinations that I visit throughout the day. We weave throughout the day, an interactive visceral experience that rarely has a predictable outcome. I know each one of my emotions as characters in a story, playing their part for me. I know them as the needles on my compass, the compass of my truth. They call to me and beckon my ear very seductively, and they will not be denied. I have had to tend to them as I would tend a garden, learning their habits and needs, in order for a hearty, nourishing, full harvest.

What's your best piece of advice that you've put to the test and now is your rule? Keeping in touch with your awareness of self, use this daily prompt: In what ways do you create and hold emotional space for yourself?

Next, I want you to consider this statement: If you don't start where you are, you can never end up where you dream.

Lastly, consider this question: Do you have a specific emotion that rises up more frequently than any of the others?

I ask myself this question before bed, and much of the time, my witchy self just sends me some unlocked, magical stuff via my dreams.

I have a small set of rules when working with myself via prompts and questions. They are designed to get you communicating with yourself and processing your feelings, not making judgments or assessments on them:

- No shame
- No "shoulds"
- Feeling into my body and having the conversation with whatever arises with compassion and gentleness
- Becoming and embracing myself as the friendly witness

Use your daily prompt, start and end your day with an affirmation. You'll set the tone for your day, you'll bring awareness to yourself, and you'll enable your dreams to figure out some shit for you while you sleep, daydream, or wait in line for coffee.

The greatest source of your suffering are the lies you tell yourself. You will never "get better" without knowing what you know and feeling what you feel. You can heal what you can feel.

Similarly, you can only experience the heights of joy and happiness when you are aligned and in balance.

Emotions can guide or hinder us, and when we are able to decipher what is causing those emotions, that is when we are able to be true to ourselves and what we need out of life. That is when we can feel them, let their experience flow through you, and inform you on what direction you should take. Think about emotions like those little lights on the dashboard of your car – indicators of what you should pay attention to in your body.

THE GPS OF YOU

"It's not the load that breaks you it's the way you carry it."
—C.S. Lewis

In retrospect, I was stripping under the guise that I was empowered in some form or another. I gave myself the illusion that I was in control. I showed up on my own terms, I had pussy, and someone else wanted it. I got to say how and when. It was also a way to keep me from taking stock of what I really truly valued. I didn't have to go deep, and therefore I became devoured by my paralyzing fear that I was worthless. I thought what I needed was money, and a shit ton of it!

I thought I didn't have the time to connect the dots. I knew something wasn't quite right.

I thought that I would always have work. Sex sells, and it would always be that way. It has been that way for hundreds of years, and history repeats itself. To me that was very important because it meant job security. Don't get me wrong, there is a name for the stripper who is still in the game at forty-five, unfortunately, and I honestly told myself I would never be that woman. I could have easily been this beautiful woman who learned to endure at a level I could not have understood, though just like I ignored the impact of my toxic environment, I also didn't consider that as a possibility. I was really holding a lot of the collective shame as if it were my own, as if I had some right to own it all unto myself, unconsciously, of course. I was hiding from myself and others in my life.

So when it came to understanding my needs, I simply took care of what I was selling: my body and my looks. That was all that occurred to me, and frankly I couldn't afford to contemplate any other way of thinking. I had to survive what was in front of me.

I was busy holding on to my people-pleasing behaviors and caring for people who did not see me. I was empathetic with clients as a fair exchange for money. I had a lack of personal worth. It is just that simple. When I look back on it now, who was setting my wages? It wasn't me. I started where the "man" told me to start. And in my case, it was a woman!

All of those men whom I thought I was "playing" or "manipulating" – albeit with their consent and awareness – were all part of the fantasy. I was a commodity, and the real game was funneling the money to a good ol' boys club, or "established assholes united," which I hadn't even noticed. My self-esteem was fanned by delusions of grandeur. I just had so much desperation at the soul level that I had no sight.

Fast-forward several years. I have paid a lot of money and life lessons to know what I know for myself. I share with you my process of how to locate what your needs are and how to execute your energy on meeting them.

Becoming connected and assured in your needs and values will allow you to make more informed and aligned choices, allowing you to take more control of your life. This means that you are building a life instead of just living one.

Being authentic is paramount to this process. As you try to evaluate your needs and values from a fresh perspective, consider how you would like to feel. This is sometimes referred to as a core desired feeling. This feeling represents something that just lights you up. You feel it deep inside you.

VALUES VERSUS NEEDS

Values tend to be long term, and fairly fixed. They don't change very often, and when they change, they usually don't change much. They should determine your priorities. They are the measure many of us use to tell if our life is turning out the way we want it to. When the things that you do and the way you behave match your values, life is usually good. You're satisfied and content. But when these don't align with your personal values, that's when things feel wrong. This can be a real source of unhappiness. This is why making a conscious effort to identify your values is so important. Take some time out and remind yourself of what's really important to you. If you are not sure what I am referring to, just ask yourself these clarifying questions.

1. Are your activities in keeping with those values?
2. Do you feel good about what you do, how you are behaving, who you keep company, how you express yourself, or how you treat yourself?

It's good to check in once in a while to make sure that your life is in line with what you believe is really worthwhile. It's easy to get on life's treadmill and lose track of its meaning. Taking regular breaks to identify your core values and realign yourself with them if necessary. Make doing this a priority.

Needs, on the other hand, are dynamic and are very contextual. They might apply to the long term, such as a need to feel loved.

But they can often be very immediate like the need to get out of this club right now, because I don't feel comfortable or safe. Once you're away from that situation, the need often changes or is gone completely.

Similarly, when your needs or values aren't met, they send different signals. When you are misaligned with your values, it's not always readily apparent. Sure, if you're confronted with a choice that directly opposes your values, you will notice. But most often, there's only a vague sense of malaise, discontent, anxiety, or sadness that you can't quite put your finger on.

Contrastingly, unmet needs are usually much more apparent, and they are often manifested in complaints, lashing out, or taking action. For example, if you're tired, you might share with your BFF that your roommate is "super rude," when really she just gets up earlier than you. You haven't been getting to bed at a regular time, and you haven't found a routine that works for you yet. It still might take a while to get address the root of your problem.

DISCOVERING YOUR VALUES

First, I identify what is important to me by way of establishing my personal values. Personal values or core values are the fundamental beliefs of a person and represent what you believe is important to you, covering all the aspects of your life.

These values will inform you about your goals, assist you in creating them, inform you on how to prioritize them, and lastly, what it will take to achieve them.

Values can be defined as "Discerning the relative importance of things to you in each of the areas of your life." It's all based on what factors you trust in when you evaluate choices. Here's a really simplified example. Let's say you're going to buy a new jacket online. Everything else being equal (features, functionality, etc.), which of these would be most important to you: Brand name? A photo of the product? A recommendation from a friend?

We use similar criteria when making personal choices, although much of the time, we're not very aware or deliberate about it. Use these questions to identify your core values, and increase your awareness of what drives your choices.

- Who do you want to be in your life?
- What matters most to your heart?
- What personal strengths or qualities do you want to develop?

Values are not about what you want to get or achieve; they are about how you want to behave or act on an ongoing basis.

Here are ten core values from a larger list in the book *The Happiness Trap* and ACT therapy.

1. Acceptance: be open to and accepting of myself, others, life, and so on.
2. Adventure: be adventurous; actively seek, create, or explore novel or stimulating experiences
3. Assertiveness: respectfully stand up for my rights and request what I want
4. Authenticity: be authentic, genuine, real; be true to myself
5. Beauty: appreciate, create, nurture or cultivate beauty in myself, others, the environment.
6. Caring: be caring toward myself, others, the environment.
7. Challenge: keep challenging myself to grow, learn, improve.
8. Compassion: act with kindness toward those who are suffering.
9. Connection: engage fully in whatever I am doing and be fully present with others.

10. Contribution: contribute, help, assist, or make a positive difference to myself or others

Assess each of those values from one to five based on how important they are to you. Then take the top five as they represent your values.

Once you have these values clear you can always come back to them when making a life decision or when you would like to improve some area of your life.

Having your values clear is one way to own your power. I find that it is energizing and does support me in enumerable ways to be a success in making transformational changes in my life. Becoming clear gives you true information to work with regarding the future you want to create.

With time, you will see how this has the potential to keep on your own personal path to your freedom on your terms.

For the complete list and some printable worksheets, please visit my website http://angelinalombardo.com/love-letters/resources.

DETERMINING YOUR NEEDS

Most of what I have learned about my needs was a result of becoming clear about my reality and what I received from practicing eastern meditation principles.

You've probably heard about Maslow's Hierarchy of Needs. Its premise is that our focus and effort is spent on basic needs before we can focus on needs higher up the chain. Once our physiological needs (such as food and shelter) are met, we can focus on security; then love and belonging, esteem; and ultimately self-actualization. There are many variations on this work, and many that disagree with it.

The most important part that concerns us is to understand that it can be very difficult to answer some key internal questions about what we desire and where we belong if our basic needs aren't met. For exotic dancers, it can be very challenging to feel safe in an environment where there is rampant abuse and often bouncers are required to keep patrons from jeopardizing safety. In that environment, how can you properly assess and ensure your need to love, be loved, and belong is met? How can you make sure you're aligned with whatever your soul is calling you to do?

TYPES OF NEEDS:

- Acceptance
- Accomplishment
- Acknowledgement
- Adventure
- Attention
- Autonomy
- Building
- Challenge
- Connection
- Creativity
- Discovery
- Drama
- Harmony
- Freedom
- Influence
- Intimacy
- Power
- Recognition
- Safety
- Teamwork

When looking at this list, examine each of these with the following questions:

- Which lead to you feeling the greatest fulfillment?
- Which lead to you feeling joyful?
- Which leave a bad taste in your mouth?
- Which of these feel natural, comfortable, or have worked for you in the past?
- Which of these represent struggle, or swimming upstream?

CHOICES (BASED ON NEEDS AND VALUES)

The greatest power you have is your ability to make choices. Empower your future through decisions. You have a say in life. You are not who you think you are.

Many of us are on achievement autopilot. We follow a course based on a limited set of available jobs, college majors, or life scripts passed to us by our family and friends when we were too young to choose for ourselves. If that's you, just know your why!

It's becoming increasingly common for people to change their course midstream. This acknowledgment, that we don't always know ourselves as well as we think we do – and certainly not well enough to decide at an early age what we'll be doing for the rest of our lives – is a good thing. Still, there's too much stigma applied to change: gap year, ten-year itch, midlife crisis, stripping as a temporary means to make large sums of money. It doesn't matter when transitions happen, we should constantly challenge our past decisions, and make sure they fit our current needs and values. That doesn't mean we won't ever make compromises – just that we need to be aware of them and make them consciously and deliberately. Recognize that not only do you have the authority, but you have the responsibility to yourself to ensure that your choices reflect those needs and values that you've identified.

Choices that reflect your needs and values should lead to the following sensations:

- Serenity, because you chose to take some more "me" time
- Safety, because you chose to report someone who was stalking you or who touched you inappropriately at work
- Adventurous, because you found time to get into nature every week
- Rewarding, because you made career moves that fit your values, skills, and abilities
- Competent, because you learned something new

Try to think back to times you experienced the fulfillment of your core desired feeling – that deep sensation that made you have the most joy and inner satisfaction. What were the events that led to that feeling? Were there any choices you made that led to that feeling or happy accidents that helped you arrive there?

A quick check on whether a need you've come up with should be incorporated into your life is to assess how well that need sets you up to achieve your goals. Hiring a personal trainer might not directly help you achieve any of your stated goals, but if it pays dividends by supporting a healthier, more creative, and more productive you, it would be well worth it. It's easy to see the costs of buying a transit pass as unnecessary when you already have a car, but if it allows you to spend more quality time with friends and family, or allows you to take the night classes you've been wanting to take, you're clearly providing a benefit to your life goals.

When you can identify what is most important for your needs, you will gain the power to know what affects your moods and energy levels. This information can help you reach goals, strategize and hustle yourself right outta that fucking club.

Knowing when to put your needs first–and which ones should take precedence–is a constant and ongoing process between yourself and others.

The strip club environment can't help you here – at best, you're working with and for people with good intentions that are dealing with their own damaged and protective processes. At worst, they are dangerous, life-force-sucking parasites who don't have values that are in any way compatible with yours.

So, actually there is more of a chance that people are getting in your way as you struggle to meet your needs. Or, perhaps you deny or ignore your own needs, blame yourself for being too X or not enough Y, tell yourself you are a victim of circumstance, or incorporate shame into your internal monologue.

Knowing and honoring your needs in healthy ways takes considerable inner practice – the kind that we don't get enough of at home or at the club.

Having our needs met is one of the prerequisites of happiness and health. Apart from stable Wi-Fi and Netflix, we need things like belonging, recognition, and intimacy, along with more basic needs like safety, food, and sex.

These needs are natural and legitimate. We have a right to them simply because we exist, not because we earned them or others awarded them out of the goodness of their heart.

In childhood, our parents, teachers, and other caregivers were responsible for meeting our needs. They were also supposed to give us the knowledge, skills, and inner tools to gradually meet our needs ourselves.

Ideally, this will have given us the maturity in adult life to be autonomous yet connected, to practice self-care, have clear boundaries, be emotionally present, and have healthy relationships.

THE GPS OF YOU

It will also have taught us to ask others for what we need if we cannot give it to ourselves or change our environment (e.g. relationship, work, community) if that is in our best interest.

Reality is more messy than that. Our parents did not meet all our needs or fully teach us how to take care of them ourselves. And we do not always fulfill our needs in healthy ways or even know what our needs really are, which is why we will meet people, especially in strip clubs, who will try to prevent us from getting our needs met.

In order to get our needs met, we ask something of them that prevents them from getting their own needs met. And that horny mofo who comes in with a hard on is itching for his relief. He does not care about your right to feel human.

Imagine that you want more autonomy from being "touched" at work. If the only way your client can feel important in your eyes is to assert his perceived power over your need for autonomy, it will undermine your clients need to feel desirable and wanted. Therefore, he will choose getting his needs met over yours.

Imagine you feel the need for closeness, and that you ask your partner to be emotionally open. If for whatever reason that feels unsafe to him or her in the moment you are asking, your need for intimacy clashes with their need for safety.

Imagine you ask your family to accept you, despite your chosen career, and your mother refuses you, or even disowns you. Consider that your need to be accepted was in conflict with her need to feel like a good mother, based on her values.

In strip clubs, the whole purpose is for the clients to have their needs met. So it is of the utmost importance that you are aware of the energy meeting their needs will cost you compared with the value that meeting your needs will give you. We spend so much time giving away our energy when we need to choose to use it wisely and to weave our power into caring for ourselves.

Not only can your needs be unaligned, or even in conflict, with others as in the examples above, but they can be in conflict with other needs you have. Dancing might fulfill needs for money, a creative outlet for expressing your sexual energy and identity, and attention, while being in conflict with needs to be respected, safe, and freedom from shame. Your job is to make choices that fulfill your needs without compromising others through a careful exposition of your values.

When you are able to be intimately aware of your needs and capable of meeting them, you will feel more happy and at peace. Especially when there is chaos afoot in your life or in your environment. You will have more energy to do the activities of your choosing, you will feel more motivated to make healthy choices for yourself. You are able to purge your shitty "friends" list that you may have acquired over the time you have been dancing.

It will become easier to deal with events you have no control over in the first place, if you know the value of your time, and can protect it. For example, when you have that shitty night at work, and you only made seven bucks. Come on, girls! We have all had that fucked up experience. You're not alone. You will be able to pivot with a grace that doesn't take from your energy, and care for yourself in a very unique way. Maybe you know that you need space and deserve to take the next night or two off. You will have acquired the skill of wielding your wisdom and weighing the pros and cons. Then you will choose wisely, since you can see the bigger picture. Saving, and then "banking," your empowered energy: brilliant!

WAIT FOR MY YES

"They tried to bury us, they didn't know we were seeds"
—Mexican Proverb

~

Now that you've figured out your needs, values, and choices, you're on your way to creating your life. Congrats on taking a major step toward an aligned and actualized you! Next, I will discuss boundaries, and how they will help you keep your life, and the people in it, going in the direction that you've decided.

~

For a sex worker, there might not be another subject more important to your quality of life than boundaries.

Boundaries are your way of ensuring behaviors and interactions happen within your predetermined guidelines. They are your fists of fury, your psychic mind control, your law and order. Creating these boundaries, and committing to enforcing them, will ensure that you are safe, comfortable, and cared for. Knowing, protecting, and enjoying yourself.

In addition, by clearly communicating your boundaries to others, you can smooth over potential conflicts or avoid them altogether. The important thing is to make sure you're safe, comfortable, and well cared for. Boundaries will honor your individuality and your unique emotional makeup.

OK, so here's the thing with boundaries. Everybody needs them but not everybody has 'em! They just don't. If they had intact boundaries, we would be so much healthier as a culture. Boundaries have everything to do with the household you were raised in, and nothing to do with affirmations on how great you can be. Those affirmations won't help you. What will help is being really raw and honest with yourself. Admitting where you came from is not as easy as you would think sometimes, but I can promise you this: you will never have the life you imagine or dream of if you can't be honest with yourself. If you don't start there, you will be doomed with inadequate boundaries.

Just follow this process and you will be on your way to freedom and liberation toward your right life. Thank goddess!

I want to start by stating that boundaries are more a part of knowing yourself than any psychological clarity. In other words, I am saying that you won't be able to use your mind to create boundaries as well as if you let your body determine them.

DESCRIPTION/DEFINITION

Identifying your boundaries is another way of getting to know your limits. You have all the authority. You own all the keys to the doors and windows that provide access to the outside. You need to figure out how open you want your windows to be, when you will answer the door, and to whom you will give the keys.

Boundaries are your contract with the world. They are your outer edge, the set of guidelines you'll use to interact with your environment. Boundaries can be something you communicate to other people, and they can also be rules that you set for yourself.

Any breach of your boundaries jeopardizes your personal integrity. You are a mighty and magical being, with many facets. Boundaries help keep this system in order so that all of your myriad needs, values, emotions, thoughts, ideas, and understandings can interact and exchange in a peaceful, protected environment.

Support and reinforce these boundaries by knowing their value to your core, and what they bring to you. Understand that every "no" you convey is protecting you. Also know that this makes your "yes" so much more powerful, once you know and are comfortable expressing your boundaries.

Here are few reasons why set boundaries are even more critical for people who have worked in the sex industry:

- You might be pretending to be a different person
- The audience has often completely different expectations on what is acceptable behavior
- Your environment is always more concerned with protecting their right to extract money on their terms than protecting you
- The boundaries normally afforded to all people when out in society often don't exist inside the club

WHY THEY'RE IMPORTANT

Boundaries establish a contract or set of rules on your terms that keep your interests, values and needs in mind. They are there for your protection, created to guard the conduit between your relationships and your Essential Self. They keep you safe from harm that may come from relationships, or from your past. They can help to insulate your healing and provide fertile ground for your personal growth.

You alone are responsible for your well-being, and boundaries are the foundational keys to enjoying your life. You are the master, creator, steward, and orchestrator of your domain. So if this is the case, what are the areas that concern sex workers? Physical, emotional, psychological, sexual – all of them!

I think the biggest benefit to receive from boundaries is the enjoyment you were born to have in your life. If you can enjoy life, isn't that part of expressing your freedom? We are not capable of feeling only one emotion all the time. It's a farce that one should strive for your happiness to reach a certain level. Happiness is merely one state of being that informs your experience in life.

Building resilience is a skill that will give you confidence when setting boundaries. It has a cyclical benefit. By improving your skill at setting and enforcing your boundaries, you're rewarded with a greater sense of clarity, and a safer environment which leads to being able to set boundaries that are even more aligned and effective at protecting you and creating the space that you need to develop.

RECOGNIZE AND CREATE

We all likely have some boundaries; most of them are ones that are innate, instinctive, and informed by our environment and how we were raised. In the best case, these boundaries are a good "starter pack" but are really inadequate as we look deeper and try to create more individualized boundaries that fit our unique selves as we change and grow. Boundaries go hand in hand with your values. Conscious boundaries will affirm your values and ensure that some cultural and environmental inherited values that don't represent your current state of mind don't dictate your safety or sanctity. Identifying your personal values is a great precursor process for creating your personal boundaries. Knowing your needs and desires can inform your boundaries but also introduce you to an overwhelming amount of confusion, especially if you were abused as a child. Any form of abuse introduces personal identity issues, or confusion with identification. In these and similar situations, you might have had poor boundaries or no boundaries. This is where you will find the biggest loss of power – your energy force.

I want to point out that the boundaries in the clubs we've worked in are not there for your protection in mind; they are there to enforce laws and ensure that the house gets its money. The club owners are there so that they can enforce control, so that there will be little interference. It's yet another way that their systemic control, and in some cases lack of it, is how they derive value by reducing our rights, our safety, our security, and our self-worth, and this perpetuates their power and profit.

Boundaries can be categorized into domains. Each domain needs protection and support. Each category will have a slightly different process for discerning and determining your desired boundaries.

Which domains do we have to protect?

Physical

Emotional

Time

Relationship

Sexual

Psychological

Boundaries can be set with three different settings – loose, tight, or balanced.

*Focus on an incident where you denied your Essential Self. Perhaps you yearned to travel right after high school, but your parents got you a summer internship with a family friend's business, and you've always regretted it.

Think about it. Feel about it.

*Focus on an incident in which you asserted your Essential Self. You were in a great relationship, in love, and had great chemistry, but it called for you to compromise one of your core values, so you called it off.

Think about it. Feel about it.

Write out the incident. Describe each way you denied or asserted your Essential Self and how that felt. Picture how you felt when the incident was over. Picture your boundaries at that moment.

Answer the following questions:

- Were your boundaries clearer to you?
- Did you have a more distinct sense of yourself?
- Were your boundaries reinforced?

This will help your awareness of how well you are to relating to your Essential Self. This awareness is a key requirement for setting and enforcing your boundaries.

ENFORCEMENT

Knowing your boundaries is a big step; enforcing them is another. It can be especially challenging when working in the sex industry because it breeds actual victims. Victimhood cycles are afoot. There is a prevalence of shirking responsibility and accountability around boundary setting, both due to the work environment, as well as the hard road that so many of us who have chosen that path have come from.

Though asserting your boundaries rarely feels good in the moment, it is ultimately a loving gesture to recognize someone's capability and say, "I expect better from you," or "this is the way I need to be treated." To say no is a potent medicine that places responsibility where it truly belongs and invites the other to live up to honoring those limits.

To deliver that "no," you need to learn your "no." Know that your "no" comes from a place of informed consent. You are granting someone further interactions with you, based on your rules, limits, wishes. It makes sense that these should be personal to you. We are all different and blessedly unique. Most of us certainly have the skills to start a conversation, but it's not realistic to believe that our boundaries should be known without us voicing, expressing, and enforcing them. It's either a statement that we want more personalized interaction than the basic human level, or that someone is not even meeting that low bar. Either way, that boundary needs to be heard. "No" is a complete sentence it does not require justification or explanation.

A woman who makes everyone else more important than herself cannot have what she wants. Trying to work harder instead of using your boundaries will only lead to you burning out or someone taking advantage of you. Your body knows the truth. It's your best ally in this game of life. It will tell you the truth in any situation without betrayal. It's right every single time.

A few chapters ago, I mentioned a session with my therapist, as she got really close and asked me to let her know when I felt comfortable – using sensations in my body, not with my mind. We discussed how your body often has extra, different, valuable information about your situation that you need to learn to tune in to. That felt sense, that body wisdom, is extremely effective at informing your boundaries, and will often be the first trigger you notice when your boundaries are violated.

I want you to think of the effect it has to pretend you're different than you really are. Now, it's not going to take too much to use that imagination since that's what a sex worker's job is, selling fantasy, something that is abstracted so it fits into the minds of the patrons and clients in those dark corners. For the client, even though they are a party to this transaction, they are not part of what is happening inside of you. To be someone that you're not lets alien behavior and attitudes enter your boundary, and that leads you to abandon your true self.

I was already stripped of my sense of self due to the household in which I was raised. I had no idea how disempowered I was when I started dancing. I even actually thought I was empowered. Only later did I realize that though I was indeed fierce, I just never had a chance to develop my true nature. If I could wave my magic wand, I'd show you all of the reasons you deserve to figure this out as soon as these pages turn in your hands. Wounded healer activated...

If you are on a path with compromised or absent boundaries, I am calling for you to not continue. no more pussyfooting! Your best you is counting on you.

A FLOAT TANK FOR WHENEVER

"The woman who follows the crowd will usually go no further than the crowd. The woman who walks alone is likely to find herself in places no one has ever been before."

—Albert Einstein

Deep down you already know the truth...cause you ARE the truth.

TAKING CARE OF YOUR SHIT

You're no normal goddess. You're a bona fide, fierce ass fighter, right? Firstly, hell to the yeah! Secondly, if you're anything like me, like most people, that fierceness isn't 24/7. And even if it was, well, that fierceness can get you into trouble or at least blind you to trouble you'd otherwise be able to identify. Self-care is paramount in keeping you able to show up, avoid trouble, achieve your goals, maintain the healthy perspective and balance to have great positive relationships. Your life gets so much better when you're ensuring that the best you is online and ready for action.

—

A woman who is out of touch with her own body can NOT have what she desires.

—

Self-care not only requires learning and practicing some techniques and strategies to leave you balanced and effective physically, emotionally, mentally, and spiritually. It also demands that you listen and understand those signals that are sent to you, letting you know where we need to focus your care. It's even more critical as a woman in this imperfect world. If you have a history of working or living in an environment with shame, abuse, or neglect, then self-care becomes even more important, because you are often not in a place where you'll get it easily.

Self-care also requires that you think through your goals and priorities because the plan that you draw up will need to take those into account.

The great thing about self-care is that there is a circular pattern at play. As you get better at taking care of your needs, you discover other needs and bring yourself into greater balance. This is related to the hierarchy of needs, but as you can imagine, it's not really a linear process. Each day brings new challenges and experiences. Situations that might cause an unbalanced you to go into code-red mode might be easily navigated once you've got a strong foundation in place.

There are many reasons why we don't take care of ourselves properly. We might not think we have the time. We don't think we have the money. We don't think we understand our needs accurately. We think we aren't in the mood. We think it's not a priority. Or we think we don't deserve it.

Sometimes we even try to take care of ourselves, but we often follow someone else's plan, or desire some learned or cultural rewards that just don't replenish us like we need to. Now that you've gotten a glimpse of what to look for, how to understand your feelings, and listen to your body, you can build a much more complete list of things that you can indulge in to keep you operating in an optimum way.

Another reason why we need self-care is to ensure that we're our own first friendly witness. Whether it's through thoughts and reflections of things that have happened, or new situations, it is critical to create the environment that will hold ourselves, and give us room to fall, fail, hurt, ache, and even succeed. There are so many learned behaviors and inhibitors that block us from properly feeling those events so that we can move on from them!

A woman who cannot take care of her temple cannot have what she wants.

SELF-CARE CHECKLIST:
BODY AND ENVIRONMENT

- Skin, hair, health, oils
- Clothes
- Shelter, smell, sound
- Massage, chiropractic, acupuncture
- Diet
- Fitness
- Sex

TIME AND SCHEDULE

- Routines, patterns, habits
- Efficiency
- Money versus time – know your value

PLANS AND PRIORITIES

- Meditation
- Travel
- Indulgences

ENERGY

- Toxicity audit (relationships, location, work, friends)
- Boundary awareness/audit – are you saying no?
- Are you living according to your personal economy and values?

The items in the list are intentionally generic. You will need to personalize them. Inject them with any and all details you need so that you feel like it's a roadmap for reminding you to take care of you. You likely already have a version of this list, but it's incomplete and probably just composed of the things that you can squeeze in when you have time off or no plans.

By giving it just a little more structure, and a little more detail, you're showing yourself that you take seriously the responsibility of taking care of yourself. You're showing yourself that taking care of you is a priority. Self-care should be planned and arranged so it's not the thing that gets missed if you take an extra shift or go out with friends.

A SQUAD-BASED STRATEGY FOR THE SHIT STORM

"You are far too smart to be the only thing standing in your way."
—Angelina Lombardo

Change can be challenging enough on its own. But implementing change is a totally different animal when life is doing its standard operating procedure of being unpredictable. It's impractical to prepare for every inevitability, every outcome, any surprise waiting around the corner. But that doesn't mean you can't anticipate the unexpected and know where to go when challenges come your way. Having an approach to manage these obstacles, whether minute or massive, will give you confidence and steel your spirit so that you can confront challenging goals and try new things without being afraid of failure.

I have made fear a friend and partner – a supporter of my highest order or path. The saying goes *feel the fear, do it anyway*. But if you lack a relationship or connection to that fear how will you approach it? With doubt, despair, or confusion? In order to forge ahead on your truest path in your life we must make companions of all our emotions and all of our faculties. We must work to connect with our breath – it connects us directly to our inner wisdom. It's like your mobile phone. On the other side is the cosmic mystery that is life where your inner wisdom is just waiting to talk to you. It comes in loud and clear, and you will have no doubt when the wise words are felt deep in your soul. This stillness where our fear is modulated is one of the ways in which your bravery is called into action.

Failures happen for all sorts of reasons and are often out of our control. There are two ways to minimize the effect that failures have on us: we can either anticipate and avoid failures or accept and navigate around them without making them any bigger. So embracing failure, having a plan to take care of yourself when you find it and addressing it head on is your recipe for engaging it.

Like change, failure is an opportunity for growth. We often undergo the greatest transformation when confronted with crisis. Accepting that primal power, you can actually accelerate your velocity toward achieving your goals through failures instead of letting them derail you. Some situations will call on your ability to adapt, and some will require dogged determination, but in either case, confident persistence is your ally.

It is your ability to be honest with yourself that is so very crucial to so much of this process. Know what drives you. Understand why each goal, each investment, each relationship is aligned with who and what you want to be. You'll have the energy to push through a metric ton of failure if you are keenly aware and aligned with your goals. You will find a reservoir of patience and resolve as you push through, becoming more skillful in each attempt. Many things take effort, time, and persistence, but they will seem smaller as your confidence in your process and your closeness to your inner truth grows.

I talked about how personal your process is, and while most of your inner work takes place in solitude or with a coach or therapist, you are also continuing on with your life. And so often, concepts, ideas, processes, thoughts, emotions, and intuitions that make sense when we're alone don't seem so simple when we're out in the world. Make some time to review and reinforce your process; allow some wiggle room for when it doesn't make sense when out in the world. Accept that it's not perfect and may need clarification, but don't rush to throw it out yet.

Interacting with people, especially those with whom we have close relationships with can be the biggest test of your process. You might want to alter some relationships to bring them in closer alignment with your new choices and values, and some people might not be ready. For others, you might choose to stop your relationship if you're realizing that they aren't positive or draining your energy. You might choose to seek new relationships that fulfill some newly identified needs and priorities. Trust your process, and fill your left pocket with patience and your right pocket with boundaries.

It might be tempting, but don't cling to safety from connection with humans. You need your process to work for you. You need it to be integrated with your life and stand up to those unpredictable tests that seem to happen much more often on Mondays. It's important to increase your capacity to tolerate confusion. Sometimes you'll be able to thoughtfully reduce your confusion, and other times you'll be able to weather it by clinging to those thoughts and parts of your process that help you stay grounded.

If you are struggling with an addiction, unhealthy habits, or behaviors, and they are part of your process, understand that even a profound change in every aspect of your life won't eliminate many of the neurological and physiological patterns you might have learned. Have patience, seek help where you need to, and monitor those changes separately from the larger process you've committed to. The changes your making will help you, but not all at once. Be gracious with yourself.

SHAME REVISITED

For us, shame looms large as our biggest obstacle. The strongest of women need the greatest commitment to self-care, as often times there are layers of shame that are deeply wound within our beliefs. Shame is very toxic, and will have you twisted and hiding in no time, and along with that comes self-neglect.

Here's the deal with shame - you are not exempt from it if you are human - period. We all have shame, whether we are in the sex industry or not. It does not play favorites, and it is one of the most primitive emotions we experience. Shame, I believe, drives from a fear of disconnection. Since we are hardwired for connection - all of us are - it is this fear of being ridiculed, left out, or just plain left that will have us doing our best to control how we appear to the outside. You may think that shame is reserved for certain circumstances, such as being a sex worker, but the fact is, shame is in the everyday. Shame has you believing that you are bad, and guilt will have you feeling you did something bad. It's in your negative self-talk that you will find shame hiding out, so use this distinction to see where your biggest areas of shame are lurking.

The less we talk about shame, the more control it has over our lives. It seems to me that telling ourselves that we are "strong" comes from an attempt to reassure ourselves instead of true personal strength. This can really trip you up, as you explore your shame.

The simplest way I know to combat shame is to find your friendly witness. This needs to be someone you trust and are 100% safe with. Shedding some light on shame, and the various ways it interferes - whether to suppress your spirit, lead to your fulfilling a role, or attacking your self-worth - is the only way to move past it. If you're in need of a friendly witness, I'll reiterate what I said earlier - I'm here for you, and you can reach me through my angelinalombardo.com/lets-talk.

Lastly, while your persistence and vigilance are absolutely assets you need to leverage during this change, make sure to avoid Inner Work Burnout by just shutting things down and indulging in something that takes care of you. Have confidence that you'll pick your work back up when the time is right.

TALL LATTE WITH A DOUBLE SHOT OF HUGS

"The price of anything is the amount of life you exchange for it."
—Henry David Thoreau

Know that *you are* the one – you're it! You are taking action to bring yourself into alignment with some of your needs and values. You are creating your experiences, owning your thoughts and taking steps to have what you want. But how do you stay in that place as life marches on? Maintain, evolve, grow, and create the processes, healthy habits, and other behaviors that will keep you aligned and in control.

Here are a few more ways in which you can solidify and reinforce the changes you've so far identified.

PERSONAL ECONOMY

Your personal economy is composed of those key components that are most important to you. Your home, your neighborhood, that close-knit circle that you roll with, your art, your heart, and so on. The things that matter most to you. They are unique and distinct to you, even as they morph and adapt, ebb and flow as you move throughout time and the world.

It is time for you to guard your well-being with your life! Personal economy is more important than getting your ass in the club every night 'til Tuesday so you can take a vacation. You invest in your personal economy first, because that's where your endurance comes from. It's how you can bring home the cash and do the stuff that needs doing. It might be hard to recognize in the moment, but it's easier to replace a job that's asking you to compromise your personal economy than it is to replace a friend or family member you've wronged. So try not to sabotage those things you hold most dear.

But if you do, forgive yourself and move on.

You are still going to have problems, and shit will go wrong in your life. It's inevitable. My intention for you is that you have had enough of a glimpse into who you are and are ready for the changes that will come because you are more aligned with you and your desires and visions for yourself. You were not put on this planet to please anyone else or to love anyone else before yourself or to follow someone else's version of success, joy, and freedom. You are not here to squander your life's lessons stemming from mistakes you've made. Those are all yours, and they are pure gold when you can recognize and harness their value.

I need for you to know that you own your experience. I can guarantee you that no one will be standing in line trying to pay for your life experience.

Courage is not a word empty of feeling state – it is like a muscle. Exercise it, beeches!

Fierce honesty with yourself is one of the most crucial skills to develop when you are looking to create a relationship with your desires. We play for keeps, always! There are never doubts, just decisions. If we fail, we go again and become even more still and skillful in our search.

Whether you decide to keep dancing or leave, it's important to keep an eye on shame. Shame has a negative impact on your personal economy. Take it into account when you negotiate your salary, plan your off time, and create your boundaries. Whether it's in your past or present, shame is an indicator that needs to be addressed. If you can identify the sources of shame, you can then avoid boundary violations that may come from your world, often from directions you don't expect.

YOUR BADASS SELF, THE CREATOR

"The best way to predict the future is to create it!"
– Dr. Joe Dispenza

You are the creator! As the creator, there are some goals, tasks, and things to accept about yourself that you will have to protect when you put this book down.

First: You are the creator of your life and everything in it.

You can choose what being the creator will look like for yourself. This is not about casting judgment on the choices you've made in the past. If you want to change on the inside but aren't ready to change your life to make that happen, make sure that it is your choice. That might be the best plan for you. It's better to choose that path and be accountable for it than start a revolution you can't finish. Know that whatever change you make will be hard but that as you struggle through, you will start to feel a sense of pride in the efforts you are putting out.

Be aware of the "everything happens for a reason" rhetoric. That shit is toxic bullshit, and it leads to a huge vat of painful cognitive rumination or decoy thinking, and in my experience, it can lead to dark times and further hiding. You need to feel free to call for help, and to navigate your situation without judgment. You need to reject any attempts to figure out what is "wrong with you" – not a fucking thing, that's what.

If you are having the thought that there is something wrong with you, it is a system glitch and results in keeping and maintaining society's scapegoats, because as long as we are running around searching for what is wrong with us, the people around us have permission to keep slumbering at the wheel.

I spent years searching for answers, trying to find reasons that would bring an end to my pain. I thought that if I could find the cause, I could treat the condition. But what I found through years of searching, experiencing, and living is that often there is no reason for why tragedy has occurred.

Sometimes bad shit goes down for no reason other than we are human beings, having a human experience. Pain, heartache, grief, loss, disease, and death are inevitable parts of that human experience.

You will become more aligned with taking one event at a time and feeling your way through until some clarity is reached. Cultivating that skill of increasing your capacity to tolerate confusion that we discussed in chapters 5 and 8 is one way of accessing your power.

There's hardly ever a justifiable reason for the bad things that happen in life. Tragic loss is not laced with inherent specks of good. I got so pissed when people would say, "You can find good in every situation." That's just not the truth. There was nothing good about being raped or abused. We have to create the good, yes. We have to choose to respond in a way that brings good into an impossible situation. We have to choose to give purpose and meaning to our suffering.

You have to be the reason you choose what you will do moving forward. Here are some of the fucking incredible benefits of you taking charge and owning your power in choices.

1. It prepares you for what's to come moving forward
2. It makes you more resilient
3. It helps you shatter your old beliefs
4. It helps invite progress, not perfection
5. It makes you more empathetic and authentic

Some of those were, and continue to be, my *whys* for creating lasting transformation in my life.

Some of these choices we make consciously, some unconsciously, and some feel more like discoveries than choices. Listening with receptive imagination to discover what to do next is one of the most important life skills we have.

And even though some tragic events happened, and may happen again, they can't be excuses that you can allow to rule your life now that you have read this book. Stick to your guns, gurl; you are a badass boss bitch. Get it right! You're just waiting to know that!

You are, in fact, already creating change, so we know you can do it. Sometimes that change may look negative or like a limited opportunity: example, obsessive creation and workaholism. That doesn't feel very good does it?

Side note: Sometimes we feel that we are not in control of what is happening to us – for instance, in the case of an oppressive or discriminatory social system or a dysfunctional family. And although you might have created the experience of going to jail if you broke a law, that does not mean you created the current reality of the prison system. Much of our lives are created collectively, not individually.

Keep an eye out for how you are creating that for yourself and own it, so you can move on. Simply stated, if you notice that you've created a negative circumstance for yourself, acknowledge that you are doing that and forgive, release, and focus on your next play.

A crisis can present in many different forms, from the death of a loved one, to loss of a job, to collapse of a marriage, to financial disaster. When you are hit by a crisis, an emotional storm is likely to whip through your mind and body, tossing painful thoughts and feelings in all directions.

Here's what you can do to survive and thrive: STOP.

- Slow your breathing: Take a few deep breaths, and mindfully observe the breath flowing in and flowing out. This will help to anchor you in the present.
- Take note: Take note of your experience in this moment. Notice what you are thinking. Notice what you are feeling. Notice what you are doing. Notice how your thoughts and feelings are swirling around and can easily carry you away if you allow them.
- Open up: Open up around your feelings. Breathe into them and make room for them. Open up to your thoughts too – take a step back and give them some room to move, without holding on to them or trying to push them away. See them for what they are and give them space rather than fusing with them.
- Pursue your values: Once you've done the above three steps, you will be in a mental state of mindfulness. The next step is to respond to the crisis by pursuing a valued course of action. Connect with your values: ask yourself, "What do I want to be about, in the face of this crisis? What do I want to stand for? How would I like to act so that I can look back years from now and feel proud of my response?"

Things to Consider:

1. Do you need, or would you benefit from, help/assistance/ support/advice? If so, what friends, neighbors, or relatives can you contact? What professionals could you arrange to see?

2. Have you experienced anything similar before? If so, how did you respond in a way that was useful and helpful in the long term? Is there anything you learned from that experience that you can usefully apply now?

3. Is there anything you can do to improve the situation in any way? Are there any tiny steps you could take immediately that could be helpful? What are the smallest, simplest, easiest, tiny steps you could take:
   a. In the next few minutes
   b. In the next few hours
   c. In the next few days

4. Note: the first step might simply be to spend a few minutes practicing some mindful breathing – or to take out a pen and paper and write an action plan.

5. If there is nothing you can do to improve the situation, then are you willing to practice acceptance, using expansion and defusion skills, while engaging fully in the present moment? And given that the situation is unchangeable, how can you spend your time and energy constructively rather than worrying or blaming or dwelling? Again, reconnect with your values: what do you want to be about in response to this situation? What are some tiny values-driven steps you can take?

6. You don't get to choose the deck of cards you are dealt in life; you only get to choose how you play with them. So a useful question to ask is: "Given this is the hand I've been

dealt, what's the best way to play with it? What personal strengths can I develop or strengthen as I go through this ordeal? How can I learn and grow from this experience?" Note: any painful experience is an opportunity to develop your mindfulness skills.

7. Be compassionate to yourself. Ask yourself, "If someone I loved was going through this experience, feeling what I am feeling – if I wanted to be kind and caring toward them, how would I treat them? How would I behave toward them? What might I say or do?" Then try treating yourself the same way.

THE FRIENDLY WITNESS PROTECTION PROGRAM

Without a doubt, one of the most liberating and humbling experiences I have had was during a breakdown in my marriage, and I was on my knees begging for clarity. When I became confused and enraged with trying to be the perfect everything, I let it rip with a new therapist. I had nothing to lose in my mind, and I was fucking done with appearing perfect. I was truly exhausted and completely fed up.

I was just newly married and was having some major issues with my narcissistic husband at the time. It was crucial that I have a breakthrough. I was at the end of my rope.

I had struggled most of my life with getting things as perfect as I could so that someone would come into my life and say to me that they love me forever, because I made myself valuable to them and that alone would give me their loyalty! HA! Well, it's only partly funny to read that out loud to myself, but it was so true.

I had to know everything, do everything, and be on top of everything! If I wasn't, I panicked and ran around feeling a huge sense of shame that I wasn't aware of and didn't understand. (Cue the confusion emotion definition, right?) I was completely isolated from what I was feeling about any of it. I just knew that I had to do my best to survive the shit that came my way, every day, from the life I had. I attempted to apply all of the concepts I was learning from various books, people, retreats, and self-improvement classes, as well as many mind-altering drug experiences that I embarked on.

Don't get me wrong, I had many major breakthroughs, major life-shifting breakthroughs, in other areas.

It wasn't until I had a friendly witness that I realized what was missing, what was always missing. I had no one to just listen to what was happening for me. Someone who knew how to listen and who cared in the heart for me. Not because they were being paid. I could always tell what people's intentions were with me anyway. If they were just there because it was their way of being paid, I found myself trying to be less trouble, less needy, so that it appeared I could deal with what was happening and also so that they knew that I wasn't incapable of basic human processing. Therapist boundaries are one thing, but when you can't feel the human-ness in a person, it's hard to develop a felt trust, and therefore you miss the opportunity to truly transform from the therapeutic relationship. I think it's a crucial piece that is absent in a lot of therapists' repertoire. It was a compensation for the therapist's human flaws. I paid dearly.

I was so fucking mixed up and traumatized. I had no experience of what it was like for myself to have the love and attention I deserve as a human. I deserved an empathetic listener, someone who truly cared on a basic human level, and I had yet to experience that. I had run into people who were trying to tell me what I should do or that I needed to do something else, something that eluded me, in order to attain a better mental state of me so I could fit their version of healthy.

I ran into people who were unhappy themselves; even though you would think they would know how to hold their own shit straight, that was not always the case during my therapy sessions.

Then, finally, thank goddess for Susan B.coming into my life. She was a compassionate, kind hearted, and skillful listener. It was the start of an eight-year relationship, and it truly changed my life forever. That relationship had a major impact on the quality of my life.

During my experiences of being seen and heard, I was able to actually see my own true wisdom. It was all right there inside of me. I just needed a clear mirror. And she was fantastic at her job.

WINDOW OF TOLERANCE

As you are making changes within, you will learn to recognize and protect your window of tolerance. It will be great practice with your boundary work.

Window of tolerance is a term used to describe the zone of arousal in which a person is able to function most effectively. When people are within this zone, they are typically able to readily receive, process, and integrate information and otherwise respond to the demands of everyday life without much difficulty. This optimal window was first named as such by Dan Siegel.

What I have observed, however is that as human beings we only have the capacity to stay in one state for so long before the brain and body shifts us. For example, we can only tolerate so much pain, anxiety, and fear before the brain and body respond and numb us to this excessive energy. Similarly, people will only stay in a shutdown state of feeling – emotionally dead inside – for so long before the brain/body shifts us out of this by gravitating toward (often subconsciously) things that make us feel alive. This could mean that we gravitate toward high-risk behaviors or activities uncharacteristic for us to bring about that sense of excitement, activation, and vitality. Essentially, we are self-preserving, as there is some part of the brain and body that is not ready to be dead yet.

Understanding the function of how people are responding, and what may be needed to effectively shift this emotional state, is critical for finding effective strategies to shift arousal that don't lead to further harm to yourself or others or leave you with a sense of shame. This can be referred to as a false refuge in that it provides the illusion that it is helping, but in the end the problem is still there – and it may be even bigger, and now we have layered on shame, guilt, or a sense of failure, as we have responded in a way that we didn't want to.

A true refuge is something we do for ourselves that effectively allows us to shift toward our optimal arousal zone while building our competencies, and takes care of ourselves in a manner that feels good.

CRAP JOURNAL

Another tool that can help you transition through change, is an exercise that will reinforce that you are your best chance. I call it the Crap Journal. You'll write for a month in a journal. At the end of each month, burn it! Seriously, no skipping this part. This is the shit that you don't want anyone to hear. If you don't yet have a trusted listener in your life, this is the best way to work out what you have to say without having to hear someone else say those bullshit phrases that people say when they're trying to help, but don't really know what to do or say or just want to feel like they are helping.

Just write it all out – the complaints, and the whining, and the blaming, and the old ways of thinking, and the way you self-sabotage, and your mistakes, and your shame, and your guilt, and your tiredness of being the victim of your life, and the stuck-ness. It's OK to have the thoughts you have! Just get them outta your head and onto paper, so you can burn it and release. There is power in letting go, simply letting go. No force necessary. Do it with ease. Cuss and fucking complain. Let 'er rip! And then let 'er burn!

CELEBRATE

At some point, I started very deliberately celebrating all of the inner personal milestones and accomplishments I was creating. Let's be honest, no one else knows that deep shit you have been silently working on, but when you notice the results, you should unapologetically celebrate those accomplishments. You're ready to dive deep, stand in your truth, and celebrate everything that you are – the victories and the challenges.

These will be ongoing, celebrating all of the work you do to not only change but also keep your train running on the tracks. These are celebrations you are in charge of and can feel really, really good about because they will be coming from your own personal values and are the result of your hard fucking work. You can celebrate this like you would celebrate the birth of your baby. It feels good, dammit! And I know there will be many more.

WISE & WOBBLY WOMAN MEETS WORLD

"Did you want to see me broken?
Bowed head and lowered eyes?
Shoulders falling down like teardrops.
Weakened by my soulful cries ...
You may shoot me with your words,
You may cut me with your eyes,
You may kill me with your hatefulness,
But still, like air, I'll rise."

—Maya Angelou

I hope you're feeling somewhere between the bounce back from an all-nighter and gliding peacefully above a glacial lake while getting the best mani-pedi in the universe. You should feel raw, challenged, and a little fearful – after all, you're standing on the brink of your own transformation. Yet you are probably also sensing a calm, quiet, affirming beat that comes with getting further aligned with your inner spirit and a greater understanding and belonging with those parts of you that never fit, were hazy, or even hidden. So much electricity, these times of transition, choice, and opportunity bring. You may harbor some doubts – that's so normal! Know that a buttload of super smart scientists have concluded that no matter where you are, you can reengineer your thoughts. You can become the person you choose to be.

I know this isn't an easy step. In my experience, most exotic performers get into "it" out of desperation – I know I did. Those reasons, those thoughts, they aren't limits if you choose not to let them be. There's nothing wrong with you! I find it helpful to remind myself that when something hurtful, damaging, or limiting comes my way, it's not meant to be healed; it's meant to be held.

You need to claim your best hours, your best energy, for yourself. Why are you wastin' your Zen on people who, at best, don't value you for who you are and, at worst, are those who would exploit, extort, or extinguish your light? Now is the time for tough love and leaving behind those parts of your life that aren't serving your needs.

Your journey is really just beginning – yet you're now in tune with the thrum of an ancient wisdom and feel like you're heading home after countless time away. Unlocking your greatest inner mysteries will be a continuing process, and will yield many "a-ha" moments. Embrace and acknowledge the awareness that this has been in you the entire time. You just needed the password and a flashlight to uncover them.

There are many paths from here – and I know that you're now aware that you have all that you need within you to continue on this highway to an actualized, empowered you. Still, like professional athletes have coaches, trainers, and nutritionists to help them hone their craft, there are resources for you to supplement the ongoing inner work that you'll be doing. This inner work and these external resources will work together to ensure you're connected, aligned, secure, and successful in implementing your boundaries, choices, goals, and plans.

This is a big change, and I'm here to help you retain and reinforce the knowledge, practices, and perspectives you are putting in place. While all of my clients are different, I can say with confidence that the moments just after making a profound change is the best time to engage with a coach to help accelerate and more deeply build that foundation. As a life coach, I specialize in helping people create positive changes and establish and work toward goals, be they personal, professional, or financial. My coaching is based on mindfulness, inner authority, boundaries, and being in touch with your emotions – all things we've touched on in this book. We'll go deeper and also map all of these new insights and tools to your experiences in our dialogue. In addition to my qualifications as a life coach, I am a dynamic, empathetic, super-safe place to go deep. I'm basically an intense infusion of inspire for hire!

After reading this book, you may have come across emotions, scars, or blocking issues related to your past. You should strongly consider seeing a therapist to work through those aspects of your past. A simple but accurate delineation between a life coach and therapist is that life coaches are focused on your future, therapists with your past. There's no need to put off one for the other. Both can be done at the same time. Many of the concepts, techniques, and work that you'll be doing to look inward, identify, and understand your thoughts and emotions and make choices based on that information are complementary.

Regardless of the choices you make from here, if you made it this far, I'm confident that you'll make the right moves for you. I'm honored to call you sister, and I look forward to connecting with you in whichever way our winding paths join us.

EMPOWERED STRIPPERS MANIFESTO

- *If you're gonna sell pussy shouldn't you own it first?*
- *Your worth does not equal a 20 buck lap dance*
- *Your real mystery lies behind your eyes not between your thighs*
- *Your boundaries start a mile before your curves arrive*
- *It's a job not a career*
- *A man's hand leaves a trace long after he's walked away/ gone*
- *Your motives are owned by you and it's your right to change at a moments notice*
- *Don't write for your life shitty verses just because you love the chorus*
- *Choose wisely, you can't bleach out your shame in tomorrow's laundry*
- *Be your own friendly witness, but don't get in a cycle of binges and soft landings*
- *Trust that your body-mind connection feeds your soul*
- *Make a plan to keep the hands of the man off your can*
- *Don't allow your frequent exposure to close you off to your squad*
- *Just because you can handle the shame society shoves at you doesn't mean you should*

- *Gyrate your loins for coin as a means to join with that mastermind plan to get your beachside tan*

- *Desperation is life's slap in the face, it's your opportunity to wake up and listen to that voice deep inside yourself telling you to STOP!*

- *Be proud of who you are not ashamed of how someone else see you*

ACKNOWLEDGMENTS

Susan Brown, you loved me into adulthood. I am gratefuel for your skillful, non-judgmental, friendly witness ways, for your sight "eyes," that saw me for who I am, a strong, capable, fiercely feeling, emotionally intelligent, strong ass woman who had so much fight left in her. I can't express what your counsel has bestowed upon my life, but I can show you. I am forever grateful. I will never forget you. You are written on my heart for all of time.

W, you were the first man and human to see me, and to honor my birthright as a woman and a person with respect, loving kindness, and a generosity that has taught me more about myself than I could have ever known was possible. You are a large part of why and how I have healed, and with your potentiating conversations, made it possible to find more of myself. From the bottom of my heart, I thank you for your grace, your time, and I cherish your soul as the precious gift that it is.

Shamana, before you were conceived, I wanted you, and after you were here an hour, I would die for you. Thank you for your love, and for your life. It is through our relationship that I have been able to heal my very broken inner-child and embrace her with such a fierce love. The force was sometimes very hard to bear, for fear that I would ruin you in the process, but somehow here we are, and you brighten my path still. Your heart is brave, and I know you will find your way as I did. I trust in your soul's process and journey. You were born out of me, but not to me, and I have had the greatest reward and honor being your mother. It has been, and continues to be, one of the most powerful relationships I have had the privilege of engaging with. I look forward to our future, and to watching you grow evermore into the beautiful woman you are destined to be. Thank you for living out loud and for not letting this world snuff out your flame. Blaze on baby!

T & M, thank you for being on board with supporting this project. You two are one of the best surprises and biggest blessings to come my way. We may not be blood but that doesn't lessen the strength of love that is contained within my heart for you.

Brian, the love of my life…we found each other later in life. It's turned out to be a very good thing. You are, for me, one of the most brave men I have ever met. Your love for me is palpable and delivered with a boldness that I truly appreciate and recognize. I find comfort in your willingness to be vulnerable and present with me. You are one of the best parts of my life.

To my mother. It wasn't easy, this you and me thing. You brought me in, and I witnessed you out. You were everything I wanted, and nothing I needed. You were a fighter, and I could see that life was hard for you. Whether you made it that way or not, it taught me many lessons about endurance.

I craved your nurturing as you gave it away to everyone else.

I wanted to be special and respected in your eyes.

I wanted, needed your protection and your attention.

I needed your guidance and your wisdom.

I found myself in the dark, stumbling around for the light, you were nowhere to be found.

For this, I am forever grateful.

I would not be who I am today if you weren't who you showed up to be for me in this lifetime. I love myself sumthin' fierce. I recognize some of your spirit in me. Your boldness, your ballsyness. I forgive all of the times you tortured us, abused us in ignorance, turned your back on the horrors I experienced at the hands of all of my sexual abusers, the times when you chose drugs or men over us/me. Abandoning us in strange places vulnerable to the hands of strangers, and for the many countless acts of violence against us.

I let it all go.

The moment you left your body, all of this left with you. It was a strange liberation. It has been the biggest heartbreak of my life, this you and me thing.

ABOUT THE AUTHOR

Angelina Lombardo is a professional and personal life coach. She specializes in helping people identify, refine, and accomplish their dreams. Angelina has taken a winding road to her coaching career, with experience as a chef, a midwife, and an entrepreneur. Her current emphasis, focused on helping exotic dancers and other people in a shame-laced industry, has been informed by her own experience as an exotic dancer. Angelina knows what that experience is like and knows that she is called to serve that community, to help them achieve their goals, and develop their body, mind, and spirit to be who they were meant to be.

Angelina has been mentored by some amazing and successful leaders, including Martha Beck, Susan Hyatt, and Angela Lauria. *Love Letters to a Stripper* is her first book.

Angelina currently lives in Seattle, WA within earshot of her lovely daughter, though during the rainy season she considers Maui home. She loves traveling and Long Distance Love Bombs, is a bad ass in the kitchen, will give you a run for your money singing karaoke, and needs stand-up comedy in her life, though not necessarily in that order.

THANK YOU

Thanks so much for reading *Love Letters to a Stripper*! The fact that you have gotten to this point in the book tells me something important about you: you're ready. This isn't the end, but rather the beginning of a life changing and worthwhile future. I sincerely hope that this book has provided you with peace of mind and encouragement as you plan your possible departure and ditch the desperation as an exotic dancer.

Lastly, I have created a four-part video series that goes into greater detail on some of the more advanced topics we've discussed here on my website. Go to the link below and I can't wait to hear from you! http://angelinalombardo.com/love-letters/resources